FAMINE

A Heritage of Hunger

Guides to Contemporary Issues

Richard Dean Burns, Editor

This series is devoted to exploring contemporary social, political, economic, diplomatic and military issues. Each guide begins with an extended narrative which introduces opinions and interpretations regarding the issue under discussion, and concludes with a comprehensive bibliographical survey of the essential writings on the topic, including recent articles, books, and documents. The guides, consequently, are designed to provide reference librarians, academic researchers, students, and informed citizens with easy access to information concerning controversial issues.

This series has been developed, in part, in cooperation with the Center for the Study of Armament and Disarmament, California State University, Los Angeles, California.

#1 THE MX CONTROVERSY
Robert A. Hoover

#2 THE MILITARY IN THE DEVELOPMENT PROCESS
Nicole Ball

#3 THE PERSIAN GULF & UNITED STATES POLICY
Bruce R. Kuniholm

#4 CENTRAL AMERICA & UNITED STATES POLICIES, 1820s-1980s
Thomas M. Leonard

#5 THE PALESTINIAN PROBLEM & UNITED STATES POLICY
Bruce R. Kuniholm & Michael Rubner

#6 FAMINE: A HERITAGE OF HUNGER
Arline T. Golkin

FAMINE

A Heritage of Hunger

A Guide to Issues and References

Arline T. Golkin

REGINA BOOKS
Claremont, California

Library of Congress Cataloging in Publication Data

Golkin, Arline T. (Arline Tartus)
  Famine, a heritage of hunger.

  (Guides to contemporary issues; 6)
  Bibliography: p. 117.
  Includes index.
  1. Famines. 2. Food supply. 3. Food relief.
I. Title. II. Series. [DNLM: 1. Food Supply. 2. Hunger.
3. Starvation. WA 695 G626f]
HC79.F3B63 1986   363.8   86-26138

ISBN 0-941690-21-0
ISBN 0-941690-20-2 pbk.

The cover design is from a photograph by Mary Ellen Mark which originally was published, in color, on page 124 of "Cry, the Pitiless Land" *Life* 8:5 (May 1985): 124-134.

Regina Books
Box 280
Claremont, CA 91711

Manufactured in the United States of America

Contents

MAPS

Preface

The purpose of this study is to explain past and present famine problems, to examine relief, rehabilitation and prevention mechanisms, and to explore issues raised by the ongoing search for means to cope with, and eliminate, famine conditions. The issues which surround the subject of famine are complex and often controversial because the disorders which produce famine conditions are long-term, multifaceted, and multinational.

Diverse materials on famine and related matters are included in the selected bibliography which is divided according to major topics and sub-divided according to specific subjects and issues. References to particular famines which are discussed in the main text are supplemented by additional references to famines which are not mentioned but which form an important part of the existing body of literature on the subject. The bibliography is by no means definitive. Neither is the list of famines which is included in this study. Both will remain incomplete because the problems which produce, prolong, and exacerbate famine conditions are present and future concerns which need better understanding to accelerate the quest for solutions.

The debts incurred in compiling materials for this study extend to many individuals, over a period of several years. I want particularly to express my gratitude to Professor John E. Wills and others at the University of Southern California, who encouraged research into the problems of famine in China, and to Professor Richard Dean Burns, who created the opportunity for broader perspectives. A fellowship from the American Association of University Women helped to support early research into the subject. Special thanks to my husband, Dr. Dudley Golkin, and to our sons, Larry and Graham, whose many gifts of love I can acknowledge but never repay.

Arline T. Golkin

Chronology of Famines

The following is an abbreviated list of famines recorded over many centuries, often including notations on precipitating events and mortality estimates. It is not wholly reliable, because available data are neither complete nor accurate. In most cases, it has not been possible to separate figures for deaths from starvation from estimates of deaths which resulted from epidemic disease, banditry, civil strife, or war. Sources for the list which follows include Alamgir [295], Dando [288], Keys and colleagues [273], Masefield [292], Prentice [209], and Walford [382].

B.C.
Biblical references to famine conditions are found in the *Books* of *Genesis*, 47:13 and 47:20, and *Kings*, 2:19 and 24-29.

ca. 3500	Egypt	Earliest known written record
436	Rome	Starving thousands jumped into the Tiber
272	Britain	People ate tree bark & roots

A.D.

306	Scotland	Thousands died for four years
310	England	40,000 deaths
331	Antioch	A bushel of wheat cost 400 pieces of silver
450	Italy	Parents ate their children
484	Africa	Drought
535	Ireland	Four years of famine
836	Wales	Ground covered with bodies of men & beasts
845	Bulgaria	Great famine
917-18	India	Jhelum River (Kashmir) covered with corpses
1022	Hindustan	Great drought then famine
ca. 1051	Mexico	Caused migration of Toltecs; may have originated human sacrifice
1052-60	Hindustan	Great drought followed by famine
1064-72	Egypt	Nile flood failed for 7 years; cannibalism
1069	England	Norman invasion; cannibalism

1116	Ireland	Cannibalism
1235	England	20,000 died in London; ate tree bark & grass
1239	England	Cannibalism
1315-17	Cent. Europe	Caused by excessive rain; 10% of pop. lost
1321	England	Famine
1333-37	China	4 million dead in one region
1334-35	India	Seven years of severe famine.
1344-45	India	"Many thousands" died
1347-48	Italy	Famine, followed by plague
1396	India	"Innumerable skulls rolling about"
1410	Ireland	Great famine
1442	Sweden	Great famine
1471	India	Great famine in Orissa
1486	Hungary	Great famine
1495	Hindustan	Great famine
1540	India	Famine caused by war; cannibalism
1555-56	India	"Men ate their own kind"
1557	Russia	Upper Volga; caused by rains & severe cold
1586	England, Ireland, Hungary	
1594-98	India	Great mortality; plague, cannibalism
1600	Russia	500,000 deaths from famine & plague; cannibalism
1601	Ireland	Cannibalism
1630	India	Drought, flood, war; parents sold children; cannibalism
1650-52	Russia	Floods; high grain prices; people ate sawdust
1656	Italy	Two years of famine
1660-61	India	War, lack of rain
1677	India	Excessive rain; great mortality
1687	India	War; rich reduced to begging
1693	France	"Awful famine" (Voltaire)
1702-04	India	Famine and plague; 2 million died
1739	France	Severe famine
1747	India	Failure of rain; large numbers perished
1769	France	5% population died
1769-70	India	Drought; 3 million died
1770	Eastern Europe	Pestilence in Bohemia, Poland & Russia
1775	Cape Verde Islands	16,000 died
1783	India	Rain failed, excessive taxes, wars, locusts
1790-93	India	Called "Doji Bara" or "skull famine" because skulls littered the countryside; cannibalism
1803-04	India	Drought, locusts, war, migrations
1813	Poland, Norway	Widespread distress
1822	Ireland	Potato crop failed; widespread famine
1831	Ireland	Potato crop failed; widespread famine
1837-38	India	Drought affected 2.8 million people; children sold for grain; 800,000 deaths
1846-47	Ireland	Potato blight; 2-3 million died or migrated

1847   France   Scarcity; food riots
1866   India   Irregular rainfall; 1-1.5 million deaths in Orissa /
Bengal
1868-70   India   Drought & epidemic; 1.5 million deaths
1874-75   Asia Minor 150,000 deaths
1876-79   India   Drought; 5 million deaths
1876-79   China   3 years drought ; people's faces "black with hunger;"
                        9-13 million deaths
1877   Egypt, Morocco, Brazil, Russia, & Madras
1891-92   Russia   One-third million died
1892-94   China   Drought; 1 million deaths
1896-97   India   Drought; 5 million deaths
1899-1900   India   Drought; 1 million deaths from starvation 1906Russia
                        22% of population affected
1906-07   China   2 million deaths; drowning, & disease
1911   Russia   25 million affected
1918-19   Uganda   4,400 deaths
1920-21   China   Drought; 20 million affected; 500,000 deaths
1921-22   USSR   20-24 million affected; mortality 3-5 million
1928-29   China   Drought, flood, civil war; 3-7 million deaths
1930-31   China   Flood; 1 million deaths
1932-34   USSR   Related to collectivization; mortality 4-7 million
1941-43   Greece   War; 450,000 lives lost
1941-42   Warsaw   War; 43,000 lives lost
1943   Ruanda, Urundi 35,000-50,000 deaths
1943   China   2-3 million died in Honan; 2-3 million migrated
1943-44   India   Drought; war; mortality 3-3.5 million in Bengal
1947   USSR   Drought & political acts; 2 million deaths; reported in
                        1963 by Kruschev
1958-74   Ethiopia   2-5 million deaths
1960-61   China   8 million deaths
1960-61   Congo   Civil war; no reliable estimates
1967   India   Drought in Bihar; great mortality averted by rapid
                        response
1968-69   Biafra   Deaths from 1 to 3 million
1972-74   Ethiopia   Drought; deaths from 100,000 to 200,000
1969-73   Sahel   500,000 died
1974-76   Bangladesh 1 million died
1979-80   Cambodia 80,000 deaths in 1975; no figures- 1979/80
1984-86   East Africa 2 million deaths in Ethiopia by 1985; U.N. experts
                        2-5 million deaths in East Africa by 1987

Introduction

Hunger and famine are not the same, but famine occurs only among people for whom chronic hunger is a way of life. Natural events can cause crop failures, but they precipitate famines only among people who do not have access to the political, economic, and social resources needed to withstand their effects. History demonstrates that nations with high population growth rates and low life expectancies experience famines. Nations with low population growth rates and high life expectancies do not. In the poorest countries, the rich do not starve. In the richest countries, the poor do not starve.

Past and present famine conditions have depressing similarities, as do the efforts to provide relief. While population issues remain unresolved, economic and technological development programs have proved to be inadequate. Emergency assistance during periods of acute food deficit saves lives threatened by immediate starvation, but does nothing to diminish the recurrent threat of famine whenever crop failures or rising prices curtail access to food.

The argument that existing world food supplies can meet world needs is invalid because it requires an unrealistic, radical redistribution of food resources. The notion that people should simply be allowed to starve incorrectly assumes that a demographic catastrophe can improve conditions among survivors and ignores unacceptable moral and ethical considerations.

Chronic hunger and famine problems will not be eradicated until it is recognized that they demand similar treatments. Both require multi-disciplinary, multi-dimensional, integrated, and international programs to provide emergency intervention and to eliminate their underlying cause. Such tasks are neither short-term nor simple. They require continuing cooperative research into both past and present hunger-related problems, new strategies for direct, indirect, and long-term relief, and creative measures for providing the poor and the hungry with access to food supplies and health care. Above all, they require a combination of popular, political, and international willingness to make the investments which are needed to eliminate existing hunger, avert the constant threat of starvation, and abolish the conditions which combine to produce famine.

As the following chapers develop these important themes, it will become evident that the ongoing hunger and famine problems in Africa and in other parts of the world are more an outgrowth of national and international economic, social, political, and military policies than they are a result of natural events.

I

The Nature of the Problem

The prevalence of widespread chronic hunger indicates underlying disorders in food production, distribution, earning capacity, medical care, and levels of development. It further suggests the absence of either the economic resources or the political will to improve upon them. This chapter will survey different attitudes toward population, development, food aid, emergency assistance, world food supplies and world hunger, and ideas which have been set forth in efforts to change existing conditions. The consensus which emerges gives few grounds for optimism concerning prospects for eliminating the pervasive problems of either hunger or famine. Indeed, despite massive infusions of aid from developed to underdeveloped nations, they seem to be growing.[1]

FAMINES IN THE PAST

Episodes of famine have occurred throughout history in many parts of the world. During ancient times, the worst famine conditions were recorded in China, Egypt, Greece, India, and Rome. Widespread famine conditions later were recorded in Britain and throughout Europe. During the nineteenth century, China and India experienced the greatest number of severe famines, while the twentieth century has been marked by widespread starvation in many parts of Africa as well as in Asia and India. Descriptions drawn from the past bear startling similarities to recent famine accounts and give testimony to the need for better understanding of the causes of famines and of ways to relieve and prevent them so that the histories of famines will not continue to repeat themselves.

The *Books* of *Genesis* and *Kings* contain references to extreme lack of food, sales of land, and cannibalism. Starvation, plague, and cannibalism were recorded in Egypt as early as 3500 B.C. and again in about 2180-2130 B.C. when, according to a tomb inscription found near Luxor, "All of Upper Egypt was dying of hunger...to such a degree that everyone had come to eating his children...." Famine conditions were recorded in Rome in 436 B.C. and in Britain in 272 A.D. A Russian chronicler wrote in 1215:

> O, brothers, then was the trouble; they gave their children into slavery. They dug a public grave and filled it full. O, there was trouble! Corpses in the market place, corpses in the street, corpses in the fields; the dogs could not eat up the men.

Historic records reveal that famines occurred more than three hundred and fifty times in Eastern Europe between 1501 and 1700, and more than three hundred times in Western Europe between 501 and 1500. Accounts from Hungary told that: "Famine drove Hungarian peasants to eating their children in 1505 and 1506." In 1600, famine conditions in Eastern Europe were such that "people ate straw; hay; dogs; cats; mice; all kinds of dead material." Saint-Simone wrote on popular misery in France in 1725: "the people of Normandy live on the grass of the fields."[2]

Ireland and Africa were among the areas which had serious famines during the nineteenth century. Sir William MacArthur, M.D. described the state of famine victims in Ireland in 1846:

> Frightful and fearful is the havok [sic] around me...the aged, who, with the young—neglected, perhaps, amidst the widespread destitution—are almost without exception swollen and ripening for the grave....

A first hand observer described his feelings upon entering a famine zone in Ethiopia in 1888:

Here and there, were abandoned corpses, their faces covered with rags....The dead awaited the hyenas, the living awaited death....I flee horrified, stupefied, shamed by my impotence, hiding my watch chain in shame, ashamed in my self of the breakfast which I had eaten, of the dinner which awaited me....

A survey of Indian famine records yields evidence of famine conditions on an average of two times per century in early times. According to a description of conditions in 917-918 A.D.:

One could scarcely see the water of the Vitasta (Jhelum), entirely covered as the river was with corpses soaked and swollen by the water in which they had long been lying. The land became densely covered with bones in all directions, until it was like one great burial-ground, causing terror to all beings.

From the beginning of the eleventh century to the end of the seventeenth, fourteen serious famines occurred in India, and twelve severe famines were recorded between 1765 and 1858. Between 1860 and 1908, "severe scarcity" or famine occurred sixteen times in some part of the country.

Some eighteen hundred famines were recorded in China between 108 B.C. and 1929 A.D. A missionary helping to carry out famine relief in China in 1877 wrote:

That people pull down their houses, sell their wives and daughters, eat roots and carrion, clay and refuse, is news which nobody wonders at. It is the regular thing. If this were not enough to move one's pity, the sight of men and women lying helpless on the roadside, or of dead torn by hungry dogs and magpies, should do; and the news which has reached us, within the last few days, of children being boiled and eaten up, is so fearful as to make one shudder at the thought.[3]

The first half of the twentieth century was marked by a continuation of famine conditions in different parts of the world. A letter written by an American relief worker in the Soviet Union commented on the state of famine victims in 1921:

The mothers have no milk and pray that death may come quickly....All the children have distended stomachs, many are rachitic and have enlarged heads....

Edgar Snow described a famine zone in North China in 1929-1930:

> Practically nothing was being done for the hordes of ragged, penniless refugees driven to the dusty mud-walled towns in search of food. Hundreds of last-ditchers sat or lay on the streets or doorsteps dying before my eyes. Relatives were too weak to bury them, but at night they disappeared. Human flesh was openly sold in some villages.

Famine conditions were reported from Bangladesh, Burma, the Caribbean, China, Ethiopia, India, and the Sahel following the end of World War II. The 1970s were marked by famines in India, Southeast Asia, and Africa. Journalist Carl Rowan wrote from Timbuktu in August 1973 describing conditions among refugees from the famine which had affected the Sahel since 1968:

> I cannot play the numbers game. But I know what I am seeing: flies feasting on the sore-pocked face of a child pot-bellied and deformed by hunger; children crying incessantly; their mothers wailing because their children are too enfeebled to stand in line for the sickly green concoction of pea soup and jam that is their emergency feeding that I suspect has been staged for the cameras....

Conditions did not improve during the 1980s. In 1985, Robert Kaplan described Ethiopian famine refugees who were arriving at Kassala, Sudan:

> ...they had just been through a trek across hundreds of miles of sun-scorched desert on foot and camel-back into the promised land of eastern Sudan. Many of them now had the privilege of dying of measles and dehydration in overcrowded, makeshift camps that didn't exist a few weeks ago.[4]

POPULATION

Most discussions of world hunger problems and food to population ratios refer to poor countries which have rapidly growing populations and which lack the resources necessary to guarantee food supplies or provide for public welfare. Attitudes range from apocalyptic to optimistic. The subject has been controversial since 1798, when Thomas Malthus set forth his thesis on the potentially negative relationship between population and food supply. Malthus wrote in *An Essay on the Principle of Population:*

> That population does invariably increase where there are the means of subsistence, the history of every people that have ever existed will abundantly prove.

Malthus believed that population which increased beyond the food producing capacity of the land would lead to the elimination of the surplus population either by direct starvation or by other "positive checks" that could be traced to insufficient food supplies. John Weyland, Malthus' contemporary, did not share his negative views on population increase and the prospect of starvation. He wrote:

> That in the alternate progress of population and subsistence, in the earliest as well as in the most advanced stages of society, a previous increase of people is necessary to stimulate the community to a further production of food....[5]

Many scientists and scholars have argued along Malthusian lines during recent years. Among them, Paul Ehrlich has insisted that population growth is a primary cause of hunger, that the planet is grossly overpopulated, that the limits of human capabilities for producing food by conventional means have nearly been reached, and that continued population growth could have the ultimate effect of helping to destroy civilization. Weyland has present-day counterparts who, like Ester Boserup, have proposed that increased food production is a result rather than a cause of population growth. Optimists like Julian Simon, William Hudson, and others have argued that there is no long-run limit on world food supplies, that food production will rise to meet growing demands, and that population increases will stimulate technological innovations and increase market potentials.

Frances Moore Lappé and Joseph Collins are leading proponents of a school which pays more attention to maldistribution of food resources than to population increases. They have set forth the thesis that world hunger is not due to food scarcity or to overpopulation but that it results from the concentrated control over food-producing resources in the hands of a few individuals. They further have contended that American aid to food deficit countries has strengthened power among an entrenched few and left the majority of hungry people worse off than they were without it. Mahub ul Haq and others have taken the argument a step further by declaring that, since the maldistribution of food is not global but affects only certain countries, the solution to the problem lies in a radical reallocation of the world's resources.

Still other scholars, Franke and Chasin among them, have argued that population growth is not an original cause of poverty and underdevelopment, but a self-perpetuating result of colonial policies and their effects on production relations. Mamdani explained the decision to have children as a necessary response to existing conditions; poor people need to have more children in order to overcome economic handicaps. William Murdoch wrote: "Poor people have large families because they are poor—they are not poor because they have large families."

Paul Demeny, Goulet and Hudson, and Erland Hofsten, among others, have written that population growth rates will be controlled either through development or through catastrophe. They have argued that population control without social reform will not affect the underlying causes of poverty, and that population will continue to rise in the absence of social and economic development. John H. Knowles has noted that improved nutrition and health care initially will accelerate population growth rates but that improved health conditions are the only means to promote voluntary family planning and, eventually, a decline in population growth.

The idea that prosperity produces declining birth rates is based upon evidence which reveals that birth rates have fallen in countries where positive economic and social changes have taken place and where populations have assured food supplies and access to medical care and public health controls. The shift from high fertility and high mortality, which is characteristic in underdeveloped countries, to the low fertility and low mortality which characterizes population tendencies among well-fed populations, is known as the "demographic transition." That expression has been used to describe the demographic characteristics of countries in the developed world, and to provide a contrast with population patterns in the underdeveloped world. After World War II, many of the world's underdeveloped countries experienced rapid population growth. The process began when the introduction of modern medical and public health practices helped to increase birth rates and decrease death rates but did not provide for simultaneous improvements in economic status. The poorest countries in the world are the farthest from having a demographic transition and, even if the transition process could begin at once, the time period needed for a society to move from high to low birth and death rates, and thereby to achieve stable population levels, would take from one to three generations.[6]

DEVELOPMENT

Many of the arguments which favor health care, assured food supplies, and improved economic status as means to achieve population control in the poorest countries have come to support development programs which are geared toward self-sufficiency and reduced dependence upon outside assistance. These attitudes can be traced to a conference which was held in Bandung, Indonesia in 1955. The leaders of twenty-three of the world's poorest countries met to organize the "Non-Aligned Movement" or a "Third World" of nations determined to take charge of their own destinies. They hoped to resist alignment with "First World" capitalist industrialized societies or with "Second World" socialist industrialized states. Between 1955 and 1974, the number of Third World countries grew to more than one hundred. Despite their increasing numbers, they did not succeed in altering international policies on their behalf and, despite their determination to avoid dependencies, they needed, and had to accept, First and Second World capital, technology, and food supplies.

In 1974, Third World leaders began to seek international commodity agreements and trade preferences, as well as a greater political role in the management of international institutions, under what has been called a New International Economic Order (NIEO). Neither appeals for greater autonomy nor assistance programs produced positive results. Third World debts rose from eight billion dollars in 1971 to forty-seven billion dollars in 1979, and the figure has continued to grow. Rising fuel costs have had crippling effects upon underdeveloped economies by depriving them of access to the use of technology and by increasing the cost of food imports. It has been estimated that nearly one quarter of the cost of supplying grain anywhere in the world lies in transporting it from one place to another.[7]

AGRICULTURAL PRODUCTION

The contributions of the "Green Revolution" to enhanced food production in many parts of the world are among the most impressive scientific achievements of the twentieth century. However, the application of scientific farming technology requires irrigation, herbicides, insecticides, fertilizers, and improved farm machinery to fulfill its potential. In many cases, the economic support necessary for improved agricultural production has been insufficient or absent. In other cases, prevailing market prices for food crops have been so low that they have constituted a disincentive for food producers. Additional negative effects upon efforts to increase agricultural production have included the absence of adequate food storage facilities, inadequate transport, and limited markets for surplus food. Development loans have not always helped the people for whom they were intended. Lack of coordination in utilizing outside funds, investments which enriched elites, and poor supervision of the application of funds have diminished the loans' effectiveness and denied aid to the people who needed it most. As a result, technological advances in agricultural production have not fulfilled expectations that they would play a major role in eliminating either chronic hunger or the threat of famine.[8]

HEALTH CARE

Development programs have seldom improved health care in rural areas. During the 1950s and 1960s, health programs in the underdeveloped world resembled programs for industrialized societies. Hospitals were built in major cities and investments were made in advanced systems for diagnosis and treatment. Personnel, who were trained in developed countries, emphasized therapeutic measures and massive immunization programs. They produced some rapid gains in cities. However, improvements in urban facilities excluded a majority of the people who lived in rural areas. Although services were free, the costs of transportation and lost work discouraged people from farming communities to seek care in cities.

Since the 1970s, there has been a growing emphasis upon providing primary health care to rural populations in the form of preventive medicine, nutritional monitoring and supplements, education in basic sanitation, maternal and child care, and immunization programs to halt infectious diseases such as diphtheria, whooping cough, polio, tetanus, small pox, and measles. While primary health care programs in rural areas can be costly to initiate, they are far less expensive than urban medical centers and they can reach more people. Public health experts have asserted that, in addition to basic health care, nutritional planning should be integrated into overall national development programs in countries with limited resources because it could constitute an additional means to break the cycle of hunger and poverty by getting at its roots. The costs of disease controls and nutritional improvements would be returned in the form of heightened capacities for food production and increased means to obtain food supplies. Furthermore, people who are in good health and who are adequately nourished are less vulnerable to starvation and less liable to succumb to the conditions which produce the decline to famine.[9]

FOOD AID

Regular patterns of government food aid, particularly American food aid, have been the subject of severe criticisms. Mitchel Wallerstein noted that, before the 1960s, the United States had no coherent framework for international food aid beyond the need to get rid of its own food surpluses. Overall, assistance from food surplus nations, notably the United States, has been provided selectively. For example, between 1945 and 1970 Europe received more than thirty-five percent of America's *total* foreign aid—as much as Southeast Asia, the Middle East and Latin America combined. Britain alone received sixty percent more aid than all of Africa. Much of the outside aid transmitted to underdeveloped countries was used to supplement internal food needs rather than for investments in needed improvements. As a result, it has had a relatively small impact upon the multiple causes of chronic hunger and widespread poverty.

John Cathie pointed to the deep emotional appeal attached to food aid and called it a "commendable aim." He added, however, that using food aid for additional economic and social developments is a "wide goal" which lacks clarity. When food aid is given for famine relief it is superior to untied financial aid. However, when food aid is given for general development purposes and projects, it creates problems for agricultural production, trade, and growth in both the developed and the developing world.   In other words, food aid as a form of investment in underdeveloped countries does not have the same potential for improving economic growth and development as untied financial aid which enables recipient countries to decide where they need to concentrate investments.

The disadvantages of food aid to its recipients include the potential for creating permanent dependence upon outside assistance, the postponement of independent development programs, and the negation of efforts to achieve self-sufficiency in food production. Frederick C. Cuny framed six major questions to be asked in light of the perceived need to provide food aid. First, is food aid necessary? Second, what is the social and economic impact of large-scale food programs on a country's development? Third, is the food provided appropriate? Fourth, if the food is necessary, how will it be provided? Fifth, does the provision of food aid after a disaster speed or delay recovery? Sixth, whose needs does a food program meet?[10]

EMERGENCY ASSISTANCE
    Most discussions of chronic hunger focus on inadequate food supplies or lack of purchasing power. They emphasize the need for long-term development and aid programs designed to improve food availability and health care. Famine conditions have been associated with sudden declines in food availability and emphasis has been placed upon massive infusions of food, medical supplies, and money as primary forms of emergency famine relief. However, proposals for development and health care have not been attached to famine relief measures. As a result, emergency

aid, which has become a permanent part of international assistance to underdeveloped countries, and emergency food aid policies, which have been a combination of political expediency and humanitarianism, have not been entirely successful.

Traditional approaches and institutional arrangements for providing international assistance to disaster victims—including famine relief—were examined in 1975 by the United Nations General Assembly, the United Nations Economic and Social Council (UNESCO), the governing bodies of agencies such as the United Nations International Children's Emergency Fund (UNICEF), the World Health Organization (WHO), and the Development Assistance Committee of the Organisation for Economic Cooperation and Development (OECD). The assembled representatives reached four general conclusions. First, they agreed that disasters are not isolated incidents, but development problems which require planned, long-term responses. Second, they determined that more attention should be paid to pre-disaster planning and preparedness. Third, they acknowledged that disaster assistance is a complex matter which demands careful organization and professional supervision. Fourth, they concluded that, as of 1975, existing international machinery for the coordination of disaster assistance was unsatisfactory.[11]

WORLD FOOD SUPPLIES AND WORLD HUNGER

Arguments which hold that there is enough food in the world to feed its population suggest that there would be neither hunger nor famine if global resources were equally distributed. Overconsumption by the wealthy nations has been criticized because, by implication, it denies the people of poor nations their right to food. Further criticisms have been leveled at political policies which support external domination of underdeveloped countries by multinational corporations and internal domination by privileged urban minorities. A legacy of colonialism has included increases in cash cropping and subsistence farming, a decline in grazing lands, and environmental degradation. Garcia and Escudero summarized:

There is a profound immorality at the root of the problem we are considering...but this immorality cannot be attributed to what powerless individuals do. The real immorality is to be found in the coercion, in the merciless exploitation, the sacking of certain countries by other countries, of certain sectors of the population by other sectors of the population....In modern times, there are much more subtle ways of taking advantage of initial differences in economic and political power. The power structure is the true immoral basis of the widespread malnutrition and famines in the era of scientific and technological wonders, and in the incontrovertible fact that there actually is in this present world enough food for all.

Despite evidence which suggests that existing food supplies can fill world needs, there is little to suggest a willingness on the part of prosperous nations to reduce their consumption on behalf of hungry people in poor nations. An emerging consensus holds that the only viable means for eliminating hunger and for diminishing prospects for the decline to famine lies in vigorous encouragement of self-sufficiency in underdeveloped nations. Garrett Hardin, a staunch proponent of aggressive population control measures, and an equally avid supporter of self-sufficiency, stated:

There is no survival without self-reliance, which cannot be donated from the outside. Self-reliance must be generated inside each nation, by the people themselves. There is no other way.[12]

FAMINE: A HERITAGE OF HUNGER

It is important to ask how past experience in understanding the causes and effects of famine, providing famine relief, and initiating measures for famine rehabilitation and prevention can contribute to the present and future tasks of eliminating both world hunger and the threat of famine conditions. There are no clear or simple answers. Historian Richard Robbins wrote:

The antiquity of the problem of famine does not mean that an effective or universally acceptable system for aiding the needy has evolved. On the contrary, famine confronts modern leaders with many of the same unresolved difficulties which plagued their counterparts in previous eras.

Famine is not just an extreme form of chronic hunger, but it does occur most often, and it has its worst effects, among people who experience chronic food deficiencies during ordinary times and who are unable to withstand either brief periods of acute food deficit or rising food prices.

The relationships between chronic hunger and famine, and the notion that famine is as much a health problem as it is a problem of food deficit, will be reiterated throughout this study as will examples of repeated failures to avert, relieve or prevent famine conditions. Further emphasis will be placed upon the role of diminished access to food as a major contributing factor in the decline to famine. Current deficiencies in creating programs to improve popular welfare through improved access to food supplies have profound implications for the future.

Although some experts offer hope for providing adequate food supplies on a worldwide basis, most of them warn against complacency. Indeed, a majority of the studies on future prospects predict a worsening of conditions associated with chronic hunger, and a future which will be punctuated by episodes of widespread starvation. While the authors of long lists of proposals for increased food production and improved food distribution offer reasonable ideas for their implementation, they too have qualified their proposals by emphasizing the need for the political will to achieve positive change. If governments cannot or will not implement programs designed to provide insurance against starvation, famine conditions inevitably will recur, and the nations and the people who have food to spare will be called upon time and time again to provide "emergency" assistance for famine victims.

Notes

1. Chapter VII in this study details the problems associated with chronic hunger, infectious diseases, and starvation. The relationships between chronic hunger and the threat of famine are discussed in Bang [335], Cox [297], Fisher [573], Garcia [300], Greenough [302], Robbins [569], and Tawney [479] among others.

2. Descriptions of pre-19th century famines are in Bell [383], Shea [385], Weitz [386], Dando [288], and Fisher [573].

3. Nineteenth century famine accounts are drawn from MacArthur (Ireland) [284], Mariam (Ethiopia) [397], Loveday (India) [514], and Bohr (China) [455].

4. Twentieth century famine descriptions are from Asquith (Soviet Union) [571], Snow (China) [478], Rowan (cited in Sheets & Morris on the Sahel) [331], and Kaplan (Ethiopia) [409].

5. Appleman [133] includes Malthus' writings and those of several other authors who express different views on population issues. A range of present-day opinions is also included in Berardi [19]. See also bibliographic entries 133-155.

6. For Malthusian and anti-Malthusian debates, see Ehrlich [140], Simon [153], and Simon & Hudson [154]. Some of the many discussions on population and maldistribution of resources are in Lappé & Collins [29], ul Haq [142], Griffin [27], and George [26]. Mamdani [148] and Murdoch [34] explain the relationship between poverty and growing population. The need for social reform to encourage population control is explained in Demeny [138], Goulet & Hudson [107], Hofsten [145], and Hardin [143]. On the demographic transition, see Omran [149] and Part II in Berardi [19].

7. Much has been written on development programs. For surveys of different issues, see Bauer [59], Griffin [27, 80], and Huddleston & McLin [82]. For discussions on the NIEO, see Dadzie [68], Murdoch [32], and Krauthammer [52]. The concept of NIEO which emerged in the mid-1970s has been the subject of several U.N. conferences and the foundation for a number of debates.

8. Norman Borlaug, who had his 71st birthday in 1985, won the Nobel Peace Prize in 1970 for producing a strain of dwarf wheat; he is best known as "Father of the Green Revolution." The Green Revolution now refers to increasing food production with high-yield seed strains. Green Revolution technology has been controversial because the seeds require careful management, large amounts of fertilizers and pesticides, and adequate water. The large landowners who have the physical and financial resources capitalize most on the scientific advances. For an introduction to the Green Revolution, see Poleman [34] and Cross [78].
9. For development and health care, see Austin [184], Berg [186], Solimano and Lederman [193], and Underwood [194].

10. The complexity of food aid is discussed in Wallerstein [118], Griffin [27], Thompson [126], Sommer [124], Cathie [104] and Cuny [355, 364].

11. Emergency assistance is introduced in Holdsworth [374] and summarized in Tansley [376]

12. George [26], and Lappé & Collins [29, 30], assert that existing world food supplies would be adequate if they were evenly distributed. In 1974, Hardin [49] opposed food aid for underdeveloped countries by asserting that help to the poor would bring disaster to both donors and recipients. Garcia & Escudero [301] bitterly summarized prevalent disorders.

II

A Portrait of Famine

Famine occurs as a result of multiple political, economic, social, and ecological disorders which combine to produce increased mortality from starvation and epidemic diseases. The worst famine conditions occur among people who are poor, who are already incapacitated by chronic malnutrition and undernutrition, and who are therefore the most vulnerable to starvation and epidemic diseases. Although the catastrophic events which precipitate famines are usually well publicized, the dramatic conditions which they produce actually represent a society's inability to mobilize assistance for people whose daily existence is so marginal that famine conditions can be produced by any brief interruption in their food supply.

Many scholars believe that famine conditions do not result so much from declining food supplies as they do from peoples' inability to buy food during periods when limited food supplies are accompanied by rising prices. Amartya Sen observes: "Famine is a characteristic of some people not *having* enough food; it is not a characteristic of there not *being* enough food." Kenneth Gapp argues that famine conditions have always affected the poorest classes of people:

> In the ancient world, as in the modern, famine was always essentially
> a class famine. The poor, who never had reserves of either food or

money, suffered immediately during periods of scarcity. The rich rarely experienced hunger.

Jean Mayer, Pierre Spitz, and Amartya Sen, among others, believe that famines have their worst impact on the rural poor and that the wealthy, government officials, military officers, and urban populations do not experience extreme food shortages.

Variations among definitions and perceptions of famine present a dilemma because they do not agree when a "state of famine" should be declared. Case studies reveal that, when officials fail to recognize or acknowledge famine conditions, attempts to define the problem become meaningless and wide-scale relief operations are impossible. On the other hand, William Dando has noted that the term famine is still being used improperly to attract aid for brief food shortages, and that its misuse draws attention away from more desperate needs elsewhere and diminishes support for future famine relief. Since there is no universally accepted definition of famine, and few criteria exist for declaring famine, the following discussion represents an effort to explain, if not to define or delineate, the confluence of misfortunes which shapes famine conditions.[1]

PRECIPITATING EVENTS

Most famine conditions have been associated with crop failures due to drought, flood, war, and plant and livestock diseases. Typhoons, volcanic eruptions, civil disturbances, or combinations thereof also have been held responsible for producing the decline to famine. In each case, popular distress has been exacerbated by pre-existing hunger, poverty, lack of transportation, poor communications, misapplication of available food supplies, and social and political decisions which have hindered relief to famine victims.

It should be noted, however, that while each of the aforementioned events has occurred frequently throughout the world, none of them have precipitated famines in prosperous societies with strong governments and well organized systems for providing public assistance during crop failures.

Drought

Drought produces a sequence in which food supplies and financial reserves diminish gradually. A characteristic series of events resulting from drought conditions includes reductions in the quantity and quality of the diet, consumption of alternative or "famine foods," sales of household possessions, domestic animals and land, and migrations in search of food and work. Possibilities for renewed food production are reduced when seed stores are consumed as food and when large domestic animals must be slaughtered or starve to death.

Drought need not cause famine. Areas with histories of irregular rainfall can be provided with drought-resistant seeds, irrigation, wells, and transport designed to facilitate food transfers. Overgrazing and deforestation, which contribute to aridity, can be controlled and sometimes reversed. Government food purchases for deficit zones and loans to help rehabilitate agricultural areas in the aftermath of drought can arrest starvation, help to avert famine, and provide protection against the effects of future periods of dry weather.

Flood

Flood causes immediate destruction of housing, transportion, food stores, and crops. Deaths from drowning, exposure, and disease precede deaths from starvation. Social services such as health care, uncontaminated water supplies, and other aspects of sanitation break down rapidly. Further disruptions result from migrations to dry land and, in many cases, to urban centers where people threatened with starvation seek food and shelter. Losses sustained because of flooding are compounded by the destruction of large domestic animals, agricultural tools and implements, and seed stores for future crops. Flood victims sustain additional losses of immediate and future income from handicraft industries.

Flooding need not produce a famine. Modern technology can reduce massive flooding. The silting in riverbeds can be minimized by dredging and by repairing the effects of erosion caused by deforestation. Warning systems and relief plans, established in advance of high water or storm, could reduce the economic and human costs of floods which, in many cases, occur regularly.

War

War deprives a society of farmers and impels migrations. Land may be ravaged by armies and local, regional, and national markets may be disrupted. Transportation may be destroyed or its usefulness for famine relief diminished by military needs. Combat often limits relief efforts in war zones and forces relief agents to concentrate their resources in refugee centers which depend upon distant sources for food supplies.

Although many of the damaging effects of war upon non-combatants are difficult to prevent, the idea of outlawing the use of starvation as a weapon has gained wide support among famine experts because it attacks those members of society, women, children, and the elderly, who are least able to protect themselves. Soldiers and civilians vital to the prosecution of war always are fed first.

Plant & Livestock Diseases

The most famous famine precipitated by plant disease occurred during the 1840s, when potato blight destroyed the dietary mainstay of the Irish people. Had Ireland maintained a multiple crop agricultural system, or had the British government not insisted upon exporting available supplies of wheat, oats, cattle, pigs, eggs and butter, the hardship and death toll would have been lessened. A livestock disease (rinderpest) destroyed three-quarters of the cattle in Ethiopia during the 1880s and ninety percent in the 1890s after it was introduced, inadvertently, by Europeans. Some thirty percent of the people died because they could not produce food without animals and because they did not have the means to replenish their herds.

Different forms of plant and animal diseases still threaten food production. However, most of them can be controlled and both agricultural diversity and improved animal husbandry can provide insurance against their impairing total food production.[2]

UNIVERSAL FEATURES OF FAMINE

No two episodes of famine have ever been identical and no two societies have ever responded to famine conditions in the same way. Nonetheless, certain phenomena have occurred with sufficient regularity to suggest some universal features of famine.

The most prominent signs of famine are widespread death from starvation, social disruption, and the spread of epidemic diseases. However, famine is a multifaceted process with additional and less dramatic signs and responses which both precede and accompany the more sensational indicators. They include changes in eating patterns, declines in the demand for employment, hoarding of food supplies, and profiteering by merchants. Food prices rise. Personal possessions and property, such as household goods, tools, domestic animals, and land, are sold to buy food. They may never be recovered. Markets disappear. Seeds needed for the next year's planting are eaten, sold or destroyed. Increasing debilitation and death within the human and animal work forces, as well as population migrations, diminish prospects for renewed food production. Marriage and birth rates decline, while mortality rates rise. As the social order breaks down, people in famine-stricken communities resort to virtually any activity to obtain food. Theft, brigandage, prostitution, progressive abandonment of the sick and immobile, migrations in search of work and food, sales of women and children, and cannibalism have been recorded.

Economic status can alter the effects of famine upon different individuals and groups. When crop failures cause food supplies to become very scarce or very expensive, the wealthy are able to buy available food or they can move to areas of plenty. The people who suffer most from famine are those who are least able to maintain adequate subsistence levels during ordinary times. Ironically, wealthy members of famine-stricken communities can increase their wealth by purchasing land, animals, and possessions at depressed prices.

Although associations have been made between famine and revolution, famines have rarely stimulated upheavals. Rebellious activities such as food riots or looting may occur during the early stages of famine, but people facing starvation are too weak and too concerned with basic survival to summon the energy or the organization needed to undertake either rebellious or revolutionary activities.

Famine mortality figures are, at best, only estimates. Despite their indefinite nature, however, they have often been used to measure the severity of famine conditions. Additional criteria for determining severity have included evidence of the inability of the living to bury the dead and the occurrence of cannibalism.[3]

Individual Responses to Famine

Changes in eating patterns may precede or accompany declarations of famine. As people attempt to conserve food stores, it is not unusual for them to reduce their meals from two or three a day to one or two a day, or even to one every other day. As conditions worsen, they may dilute food with water. Later, they mix ordinary foods with unusual substances such as seeds, grasses, roots, leaves or tree bark in order to expand their volume. The practice of consuming alternative, or famine, foods is centuries old. Sir Hugh Platt wrote of famine foods in *Sundry Remedies Against Famine* (1590) that bread could be made from the powdered leaves of pear, apple, beech, and oak trees "being first scorched and after soddened then baked." A "convenient drink" could be made of acorns and the bark of some trees. Famine foods were described over many centuries in Chinese accounts. They listed different varieties of grasses, leaves, roots, and herbs which helped to sustain life when regular crops failed and, in many cases, they warned against consuming poisonous substances. In 1920-1921, foreign relief agents in China recognized that, if they could supply grain, rural famine victims would supplement their diets with other available plant resources. Famine food consumption has been used as evidence of extreme scarcity. In present-day Bangladesh, crop failures compel people to substitute wild arums (wild calla) for normal rations. They consume the green leaves first, because the roots make their mouths and throats itch. Seasoned observers call the absence of green on wild arum plants a "sure sign" of severe scarcity. Similar phenomena were recorded in Ireland and Russia during the nineteenth century and in Africa during the twentieth century.

Unfortunately, some alternative foods have failed to sustain life and, in many cases, have hastened death. Some of the horrors of famine food consumption were described by White and Jacoby following a trip into stricken areas of Honan, China, in 1943:

> The people were slicing bark from elm trees, grinding it to eat as food. Some were tearing at the roots of the new wheat....Refugees

on the road had been seen madly cramming soil into their mouths to fill their bellies, and the missionary hospitals were stuffed with people suffering from terrible intestinal obstructions due to the filth they were eating.

High food prices which occur as a result of hoarding have been recorded innumerable times. For example, the cost of rice doubled in Bengal in 1942 and, by spring 1943, doubled or tripled again. Eventually, prices increased ten-fold. Official efforts to control them failed, and grain movements into famine-stricken areas were restricted by hoarding in grain-sufficient areas. Deaths numbered in the millions despite the fact that there were no widespread crop failures.

Stories of people in famine zones stealing food or plundering food shops are commonplace, as are the accounts of sales of women and children and reports of cannibalism. Data indicating the disruption of individual families are generalized, but available information suggests that cultural differences determine how small groups respond the threat of starvation. In some cases, elderly males and able-bodied men are better protected from famine conditions than women and girls. In others, women and children migrate toward towns to beg or to seek employment, while men move to distant farm areas in search of agricultural labor. In still others, the able-bodied of both sexes have better opportunities for survival because of their mobility and their ability to do hard physical labor.

Sales of women and children have been justified on the basis of providing them with the opportunity to survive and, at the same time, helping to assure the survival of their families. A woman or child who is sold may be able to avoid starvation in the home of strangers, while the cash or food realized from the sale may give the rest of the family a similar opportunity. Cannibalism is the most difficult famine response for well-fed people to understand or accept. However, famine records compiled over many centuries tell of cannibalism in Egypt, Italy, England, Hungary, Ireland, India, and China. The number of famines which have produced conditions so extreme that people were driven to eat human flesh has probably been underestimated rather than exaggerated.

The sale of personal possessions and property fill the pages of famine accounts. In many cases, wealthy members of famine-stricken communities have been enriched by the opportunity to buy land, farming equipment, and animals at reduced prices. A Famine Commission Report published in India at the turn of the century described inability to find work, contraction of credit, and migration as characteristics of famine conditions. The Report concluded that contraction of credit and unusual wandering of people were "danger signals" of impending famine. The same phenomena were observed in Bihar in 1967, where the cost of mortgages on land increased by more than two hundred percent and where sales of land rose by thirty-three percent. Great numbers of day laborers, sharecroppers, fisherman and artisans in Bangladesh were unable to find work during the early 1970s. They had to leave their homes and families to search for work.

Some authors of recent studies suggest that the effects of mass migrations from famine zones to urban areas may exert greater influence upon declarations of famine than the effects of famine conditions upon rural people who are unable to migrate because of starvation and disease. The idea that mass migrations influence political responses is supported by views which hold that the presence of refugees in urban centers demonstrates the inability of local communities to cope with famine conditions, and that migrants constitute a threat to the political order. Official reactions have taken form in immediate measures designed to enable refugees to return to their homes, and in the establishment of refugee camps which serve as centers for food distributions. During recent years, media reports on conditions in famine refugee camps have triggered political, economic, and social responses on an international scale.

Evidence that individuals do not suffer equally during famines is supported by studies which describe the whereabouts of the well-to-do and their effects upon economies outside of famine zones. For instance, business in China's port city of Tientsin actually improved in 1921, as wealthy families left famine areas in the interior and created demands upon Tientsin's goods and services. Life in affluent parts of Bihar went on in normal fashion despite famine in 1966-1967. While famine took enormous tolls in the countryside, business was "booming" in Addis Ababa,

Ethiopia in 1985, where an influx of foreign official delegations, relief agency representatives, members of the press corps, and other visitors created new business for hotels, restaurants, transportation facilities, and other services.[4]

Government Responses to Famine

People in famine-stricken communities characteristically turn to local authorities for relief, in the belief that their government and its representatives have a duty to protect them. Appeals do not necessarily result in appropriate relief measures. In some cases, local authorities are reluctant to admit the severity of famine conditions, because they are afraid of being held responsible for them. In others, they exaggerate needs in order to obtain more relief than necessary. Non-government or anti-government forces may distort famine reports in order to generate popular discontent. Central government authorities may ignore or conceal famine conditions in order to maintain international prestige. Ambassadors of potential food aid countries may be reluctant to transmit information on famine conditions unless they have the approval of their host governments. As a result, one of the most difficult problems confronted by local officials and governments in famine areas, as well as by local, national, and international relief agencies, has been the question of if and when famine should be declared.

The universal signs of famine, manifested in the popular responses outlined above, do not follow the same sequence for all episodes of famine. Deaths from starvation may occur over a period of months before they reach alarming numbers and, in isolated areas, they may number in the thousands before any problem is officially recognized. Deaths from epidemic diseases may not be attributed to the combined effects of chronic hunger, social disruption, and starvation and therefore may not contribute to the declaration of famine. Criteria for initiating relief measures may be vague and information concerning relief needs may be unreliable or absent altogether. National or international political interests may be used to override factual data when initiating famine relief measures. Government and private relief agencies may not agree as to the need for relief operations, and may not cooperate in carrying them out.

The following examples of official denials of famine conditions, or of exaggerated famine reports, underscore the dilemma which has confronted relief agents and agencies in the past, and which still cause doubt and confusion.

Although the Soviet government never officially admitted that famine conditions existed, starvation and disease claimed an estimated five million lives between 1932 and 1934 under circumstances which James E. Mace described as "an act of policy." Government extraction of grain harvests for the creation of official reserves, in case of hostilities against the Japanese in Manchuria, reduced grain supplies available to the Soviet peasantry in the Ukraine, North Caucasus, mid and lower Volga and Kazakhstan. On January 1, 1933, the *New York Times* charged that "hunger has not come upon the Russian land as an act of God; it is man-made." The Soviet government restricted the number and the mobility of visitors, forced refugees to leave major cities, and did not ask for food relief. An eye witness observer later described the conditions:

> The peasants ate dogs, horses, rotten potatoes, the bark of trees, grass—anything they could find. Incidents of cannibalism were not uncommon. The people were like beasts, ready to devour one another....

Crops failed in the Ethiopian province of Tigray in 1957. By summer 1958, people were dying or leaving the area, but the subject of famine was "taboo" in Addis Ababa. The government did not disclose information about famine conditions or request outside aid until September 1959, and relief distributions did not begin until late summer 1961. By then, at least 100,000 people were dead and uncounted thousands had abandoned their homes. A similar lack of official response occurred in autumn 1965. Acute food deficits were reported from Wollo Province. Migrations began in February and, by May, people were dying of starvation. However, government action did not begin until September 1966, when food was ordered into famine districts. Poor storage and transport facilities kept supplies from reaching the worst affected communities and, in many cases, shipments took close to twelve months to reach their destinations. In July

1967, corpses were discovered at roadsides. The Ethiopian government insisted that the population of Wollo had enough cash to buy grain and to pay taxes, so food shipments were designated for sale at reduced prices. In some cases, penniless people tried to steal food, but most died waiting for free relief. When Emperor Haile Selassie visited Wollo in November 1972, he was not shown direct evidence of famine conditions, but he did waive some taxes and ordered others to be paid over a five year period. Word of famine conditions did not reach an international audience until November 1973, when eye-witness accounts began to appear in the world press. Although official figures are not yet available, unofficial estimates have placed the number of famine related deaths in Ethiopia between two and five million for 1958 to 1974.

Famine in Bihar during 1966-1967 was precipitated by widespread crop failures which resulted from drought conditions. Although massive relief efforts were instituted to prevent starvation and epidemic diseases, more might have been accomplished if local, state, and national political leaders had accepted reports on conditions earlier, and if they had acted sooner. However, the Indian government initially distrusted the reports of famine conditions from Bihar on the assumption that they were politically motivated. While the relief efforts in Bihar have been praised, massive efforts were required, including international food shipments, to avert a major demographic catastrophe.

Reports on famine conditions in Cambodia (Kampuchea) during the 1970s reflected what Mason and Brown called a "legacy of concern" toward Cambodian war refugees. Representatives of relief agencies who briefly visited refugee camps saw the worst conditions, and media personnel stationed in Thailand transmitted their reports. It has since been alleged that both the threat and the reality of famine conditions were exaggerated and that, while there was great suffering, there was no real famine. In his disturbing account of relief efforts on behalf of Cambodian refugees, William Shawcross acknowledged there were real needs and recognized the problems of fully understanding them in the absence of access to the interior. However, he argued that popular humanitarianism, which coincided with political and strategic considerations, distorted the public's perceptions. The Vietnamese government denied famine conditions, and the West assumed that they were lying. As a result, donated food, fuel, and transport had the opposite political effect from the one that was intended. The Heng Samrin regime, under Vietnamese control, was consolidated with the help of about 100 million dollars which had been donated for relief.[5]

FAMINE INTERVENTION: THE AMERICAN ROLE

Private and official American approaches to disaster intervention are significant for three reasons. First, America has been the largest supplier of famine relief throughout the twentieth century. Second, American response is the standard by which relief efforts are measured in other countries. Third, the shortcomings of American private and official relief efforts have become a basis for relief experts to measure the effects of intervention and to establish recommendations for change.

Voluntary Relief

American voluntary contributions for disaster victims in foreign countries began when the Republic was formed. During the eighteenth and nineteenth centuries, American donors responded to situations which were brought to their attention by traders, church representatives or government officials stationed in affected areas. Relief efforts were neither systematic nor organized under specific agencies. Although some efforts were made to enlist government aid, voluntary patterns of giving were predominant. In most cases, they were undertaken by representatives of the evangelical missionary movement whose members did not consider themselves agents of either national policy or commercial interests. By the beginning of the twentieth century, growing American political and economic involvement in other countries was accompanied by an increase in disaster relief efforts, a widening of the donor base within the United States, and a developing concern with the causes of widespread poverty, hunger, and disease. Although, in most cases, donations were minor in light of actual needs, they did help to save countless lives and to instill in the American public mind what Merle Curti called the "habit of giving."

Private relief efforts remained generally spontaneous in nature until the end of World War I, when increased reliance upon large scale organizations, the application of business-like approaches to relief efforts, and the expanded role of American foreign service representatives in philanthropic efforts changed the nature of American relief efforts abroad. During the years between World War I and World War II, there was a rise in private donations based on commercial and economic self-interest which supplemented funds raised by religious and humanitarian groups.

Although private agencies have provided a relatively small portion of disaster assistance donations, their work has played an important role in international relief efforts. First, they have often begun relief work in stricken areas before government agencies have undertaken relief operations. Second, they have been able to provide unofficial assistance in places and under circumstances which were not open to official organizations, as in cases of civil war. Third, many private relief organizations have conducted relief efforts unfettered by bureaucratic regulations.

Private relief organizations have had difficulty achieving cooperation among their own donors and with other groups. In 1972, an effort to improve coordination was undertaken when an informal committee, known as the Steering Committee, was established in Geneva. Members included the Oxford Committee for Famine Relief (OXFAM), Catholic Relief Services (CRS), the World Council of Churches (WCC), the Lutheran World Federation (LWF), and the League of Red Cross Societies (LRCS). The Steering Committee has become an important agency for coordinating world-wide private relief activities and for exchanging information among a wide spectrum of other relief organizations. In addition, the Committee maintains communications with the United Nations Disaster Relief Organization (UNDRO) which, in turn, cables disaster reports to relief organizations around the world.

The Red Cross does not conform to the criteria for either private or official organizations. It is a movement of individuals and individual nations which is made up of three distinct parts. First, the International Committee of the Red Cross (ICRC), founded in 1863 in Geneva, has as its primary purpose the "protection" of war wounded, prisoners of war, and civilians in both internal and international conflicts. After the ICRC was established, different governments were invited to form national Red Cross Societies in their own countries. National Red Cross societies concentrate on disaster relief, public health, and welfare problems within their own borders or, in response to requests from other national societies, undertake emergency relief in different countries. After World War I, the League of Red Cross Societies (LRCS) was formed as a federation designed to assume international responsibilities as well as individual national activities. Red Cross policies are established at international conferences every four years.

Voluntary Relief & Government Policies
    Private relief concerns became an inherent part of official relief efforts after World War II, when social disorders were greater than ever before in history. In order to organize and coordinate work in both spheres, two national organizations were formed. The American Council of Voluntary Agencies for Foreign Service was established in 1943 as a coordinating body and clearing house for seventeen original member organizations. By 1947, fifty-five member organizations controlled a budget of 200 million dollars. The Advisory Committee on Voluntary Foreign Aid was organized in May 1946, when President Harry S. Truman dissolved the War Relief Control Board. The Advisory Committee was attached to the State Department and assigned the task of recommending policies which affected relationships between voluntary agencies and the government. The results of the partnership were most evident in private donations to the United Nations Relief and Rehabilitation Administration (UNRRA) and in its staffing by trained personnel from both the private and the public sectors.
    Private agencies began making plans to expand their activities when the United States withdrew from UNRRA work. Subsequently, Congress passed the Agricultural Trade Development and Assistance Act of 1954, which is best known as Public Law 480 or simply as PL 480. Under PL 480 provisions, the U. S. channeled some 9.5 billion dollars in surplus agricultural products to more than 100 countries around the world. The program, which eventually came to be known as "Food For Peace", was based upon the assumption that private agencies had a

significant role to play in overseas relief and rehabilitation and that their role could be enhanced by government assistance in procuring and distributing relief supplies.

One result of the new partnership was the creation of an agency which was first known as Cooperative American Remittances to Europe and later as Cooperative for American Relief Everywhere, or CARE. CARE was established as a means to organize and coordinate efforts to send private relief packages to Europe. In November 1945, twenty-two religious and secular agencies became members of CARE and undertook a program of non-designated giving which was characterized by skillful publicity, organizational efficiency, and the ability to send funds and supplies where they were needed most. In 1949, CARE began to use American government food surpluses as part of their relief distributions. In 1952, Church World Service and Catholic Relief Services withdrew from CARE to pursue independent efforts, as did the American Friends Service Committee in 1957. However, they were replaced by numerous other agencies whose goals were direct relief and who supported self-help programs under CARE auspices.

Government Relief Organizations

A number of donor nations have formed special agencies to deal with official disaster aid. They include Great Britain, France, Sweden, Australia, New Zealand, Canada and the United States. The United States Agency for International Development's (USAID) Office of Foreign Disaster Assistance is the oldest and largest of these and is usually credited with having developed the international disaster relief "operations room" concept.

These "bilateral" offices have been the largest source of material for disaster relief, but their actual work has usually been carried out independently. Policy decisions regarding the size and nature of contributions and the relief channels to be used have been made internally, although some contributions have been made through the United Nations, the European Economic Community, or one of several other multilateral relief agencies. Most often, government assistance agencies have contributed directly to countries in need in order to achieve maximum political impact. There has been a limited trend toward making government contributions through UNDRO, leaving decisions regarding the utilization of donations up to UNDRO officials, and letting them make final accountings at the conclusion of relief operations. The process remains fluid and depends upon individual circumstances.[6]

SUMMARY

Paul Brass synthesized six issues which have been raised repeatedly in scholarly and official discussions on the definition of famine. He phrased them in terms of issues and questions which might also be applied to the problems of declaring famine and initiating relief efforts. First, is food scarcity invariably, or even generally, associated with famine? Second, what is the nature and extent of food deprivation associated with famine, and how have terms such as hunger, malnutrition, prolonged per capita food grain deficiency, and starvation been used to describe it? The third issue summarized by Brass is one which encompasses questions about the specific groups of people affected by famine, such as whether it involves only the "poorer classes," whether it has included the community as a whole, and how each group has responded. A fourth issue encompasses questions regarding whether or not it is appropriate to use the various signs and symptoms associated with food deprivation, and the loss of opportunities for employment, as indicators for the existence of famine. A fifth question asks if it has been appropriate to use the inadequacies of traditional private relief mechanisms, or of routine government relief measures, to identify the indicators of famine? A sixth and final issue is one which raises questions regarding emphasis upon famine as a situation that requires large-scale government response.

Notes

1. Discussions on theoretical approaches to famine problems are in several of the studies in the volume edited by Robson [294], as well as in Sen [305], Gapp [384], Spitz [306], Currey [298], and several works by Mayer [324-327]. Alamgir [296] provides an excellent summary of the problems of defining famine.

2. Lists of precipitating events and discussions of their effects may be found in Aykroyd [286], Keys et al. [273], McCance [291], Masefield [292], Mayer [326] and Walford [382].

3. Keys et al. [273] wrote that "the misery of famine has always worn the same face." The universal features of famine are discussed in several sources, including Alamgir [295, 296], Appleby [497], Currey [298], Colvin [422], Dirks [309], Jelliffe & Jelliffe [312], Masefield [292], and Prentice [209].

4. Some of the changes in food habits which characterize responses to acute food deficit are described in Keys et al. [273], as well as in Prentice (citing Platt) [209], MacNair [472], Yi & Ferny (scientific discussion of famine foods) [483], Peking United International Famine Relief Commission [476], Rahman [549], and White & Jacoby [482]. Sales of property and possessions and migrations are described in Alamgir [295, 296], Currey [298], Currey & Hugo [299], Den Hartog [308], Dirks [309], Famine in India [519], Jelliffe & Jelliffe [312], and Masefield [292]. Dando [288] and Keys et al. [273] discuss cannibalism. Masefield [292] observed that the effects of famine food consumption, sales of personal resources, and migrations—as well as the debilitation of human and animal work forces—have combined to create conditions whereby "famine breeds famine."

5. The sources listed in notes 1-4 above include numerous remarks on official responses to famine conditions. For additional discussions, see Sheets & Morris (Sahel) [331], Mace (Soviet Union) [584], Mariam (Ethiopia) [397], Brass (Bihar) [539], and Shawcross (Cambodia) [450]. Green [357] has observed that governments may be selective in relief distributions to use human needs to bring groups or regions "to heel" or to resettle people in other areas. Examples of what he alluded to occurred in Biafra in 1969, Burundi in 1972, and Ethiopia in 1985.

6. American philanthropy is the basis for the study by Curti [119]. Dulles [372] describes the history of the American Red Cross in providing relief in many parts of the world. Bicknell [467] explains his role in directing Red Cross relief work. Fisher [573] and Weissman [578] explain the role of the American Relief Administration (ARA) in providing food relief all over Europe during and after World War I, with major emphasis upon Herbert Hoover's role in directing operations in the Soviet Union. American private aid is examined by Jones [121], Linden [122], Sommer [123, 124], Whitaker [127], Thompson [126], and Balaam & Carey [128]. The role of the International Committee of the Red Cross and the League of Red Cross Societies is explained in Forsythe [273], Holdsworth [374], and Tansley [376]. U. S. official aid is analyzed by Brown & Shue [103], Giacomo [106], Laird & Laird [131], Mahoney [110], and Vengroff & Yung [117]. Bibliographic entries 586-593 provide sources for information on relief and development organizations.

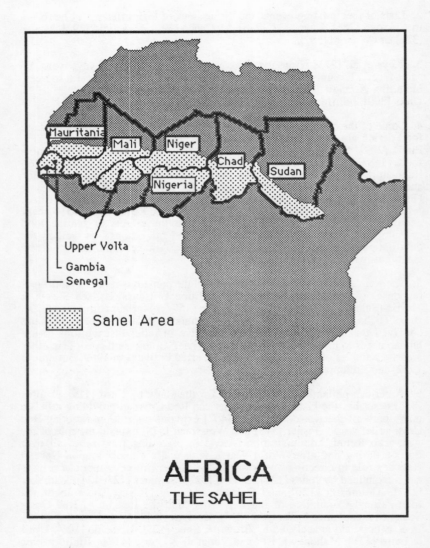

Upper Volta
Gambia
Senegal

Sahel Area

AFRICA
THE SAHEL

III

Contemporary Famine Relief

This chapter examines general categories of famine relief efforts, some of the problems which have reduced their effectiveness during recent years, and a variety of recommendations which have been made for improving intervention methods. Examples of deficiencies in relief activities illuminate the problems faced by individuals and organizations in their efforts to deal with complex famine-related problems. They are not meant to disparage relief efforts or to discourage relief donors, but to stimulate improvement of existing systems and the development of new ones.

Famine intervention generally falls into three categories. The first includes direct, immediate, local measures such as food and cash distributions, medical care and epidemic control, and provision of clothing and shelter. The second category involves indirect measures such as employment on public works projects, tax remissions, and advancement of seeds and tools for agricultural rehabilitation. The third category offers long-term programs for famine prevention, such as improvements in agriculture, irrigation, transportation, and health care. The three general measures seldom have been carried out in distinct stages. In most cases, their implementation has been determined by the events which precipitated famine conditions and by the philosophy, timing, nature, and response of local, national, and international groups.[1]

DIRECT RELIEF

Direct emergency relief is the most obvious means of halting starvation, maintaining nutritional balance, and preventing outbreaks of epidemic diseases. The major tasks of providing direct relief include procurement, purchase, transportation, storage, and distribution of food and medical supplies in famine zones. To accomplish these objectives, relief personnel must first obtain reliable information regarding the dimensions of the tasks involved. Secondly, they must determine what supplies are available within the famine stricken area, and whether existing transportation can quickly and efficiently bring supplies from great distances. Third, relief managers need to know local and national leaders who can be placed in charge of relief supplies. Fourth, it is necessary to identify normal dietary staples, to know how they are prepared, and to recognize that religious beliefs and cultural aversions exert powerful influences even among people who are starving. Finally, the pre-famine nutritional and medical status of affected populations must be surveyed to facilitate the treatment of starvation-related disorders and the pre-existing disorders which worsen the effects of starvation.

Food Relief

Food is the primary need of starving people; however, people have died because they lacked the money to buy food which was available locally, and because food shipments from outside were delayed. Therefore, price controls are essential to keep food costs reasonable and to prevent hoarding by grain merchants anticipating inflation. Communications networks must be opened rapidly and transport facilities must be mobilized immediately to accelerate food deliveries. Maintenance of law and order is a concurrent measure needed to prevent robbery and looting.

Grain rations alone are not adequate for relief diets. Rice contains only seven percent protein; corn and wheat eight to twelve percent; and oats fifteen percent. Corn and rice are deficient in amino acids. None of the basic grain foods contain enough vitamins, minerals or fat for a complete diet. Therefore, relief foods should consist of a combination of cereal grains supplemented by tubers, beans, peas and lentils, dried fish, and egg powder. Bland foods and skim milk should be available for children and for people who are closest to death. However, milk should be introduced carefully if it is not a normal part of the diet, and a safe water supply must be provided to reconstitute powdered milk. Relief foods must be packaged adequately and have reasonable shelf lives.

During recent years, special emphasis has been placed on developing combinations of relief foods to provide children with supplements of protein and calories. One such formulated relief mixture, known as CSM and developed in the United States, contains corn and soy flour as well as milk powder. Another, known as K-Mix II (Kwashiorkor Food Mix), was developed for children with signs of kwashiorkor and contains three parts calcium caseinate, five parts skim milk powder, and ten parts sucrose. One hundred grams of the powdered substances are mixed with sixty grams of vegetable oil and enough boiled water to make a total of one liter of food. The mixture is accepted readily by children because it is sweet. It can be taken through a straw or administered through a feeding tube. A Post-Kwashiorkor Food Mix (PKFM) was developed by UNICEF in 1970 to treat protein calorie-malnutrition (PCM). It contains 40% corn meal, 38% full fat soy flour, 5% dry skim milk, 15% sugar, 2% vitamin-mineral mixture, and vanilla flavor. In addition, a wheat-soy blend developed by the U. S. Department of Agriculture can be sent to famine zones pre-cooked and ready to be used for making bread.

While protein supplements can provide significant benefits to their recipients, the most important consideration in choosing relief foods remains that of meeting basic caloric needs. Geoffrey Masefield observed that it is a waste of resources to supply famine victims with expensive protein foods if minimum caloric needs are not met by other foods since the protein will simply be "burned up" to provide energy rather than perform its proper metabolic functions.[2]

Medical Relief
Since infectious diseases worsen existing hunger-related disorders, efforts to prevent or to treat them are critical to reducing famine-related deaths. Surveillance, sanitation, and preventive and therapeutic measures can be as effective as food in saving

lives. Medical and health personnel need the assistance of people who have field training in statistics and epidemiology, as well as paramedical workers, teachers, welfare workers, and relief workers. Indigenous personnel have proven to be invaluable assistants in disease surveillance and reporting. All of these individuals need instruction in how to deal with disease prevention and how to initiate treatment. Plans for stockpiling vaccines and therapeutic agents, along with lists of personnel, equipment, and transport requirements, should be made in advance of famine conditions. When a famine is declared, funds for medical relief should be allocated on the basis of surveillance reports from the famine zone. The creation of small "famine hospitals" has been recommended to halt migration, avert the spread of communicable diseases, and make medical attention available to those unable to travel to large medical care facilities.

Additional Forms of Direct Relief

In addition to food and medical relief, direct intervention should include provisions for shelter, clothing, and purified water. Both regular and medical relief personnel should be trained to assess the psychological state of famine refugees because their cooperation is essential to effective relief operations. In general, direct famine relief should be suitable to immediate conditions and fit within the political, economic, social, and cultural context of the people who are receiving it.

Problems With Direct Relief

Emergency famine relief can be both complicated and inhibited by inadequate assessments of actual needs, poor communications, poor transportation, and inadequate distribution facilities and personnel. A major shortcoming of direct relief is that it has not been carried out according to standard guidelines. Direct food relief has limited effects unless it can be provided promptly and in adequate quantities. Although direct food aid has tremendous emotional appeal, it does not stimulate agricultural production or economic growth. On the contrary, continuous food relief can create permanent dependence on outside assistance, work against development, and sustain unemployment. Furthermore, direct relief can negatively effect famine-stricken communities by diminishing local incentives for food production, damaging local and regional markets, and destroying traditional leadership by supplanting it. Phasing out direct relief can pose as many problems as starting it. An over-supply of relief food can result in waste, while an under-supply can perpetuate hardship and distress.

The different needs encompassed in relief have given rise to confusion and error. For instance, questions have arisen regarding the disposition of domestic animals in famine zones when grain supplies are at or near exhaustion. The notion that domestic cattle should be slaughtered and eaten during an acute food shortage may seem logical to some people, but not all. Nomadic patoralists in Africa look upon their herds as a form of capital and as instruments of production. Many will eat their animals only when "God kills them," and they will not slaughter them even to prevent starvation. The same groups will eat fish only when they are desperate for, to them, fish or fish products represent relief that is barely acceptable even under the most catastrophic circumstances.

Religious beliefs and cultural aversions to particular foods are often so powerful that they can override the threat of starvation and reduce the benefits intended by food donors. People in India who adhere to vegetarian diets refuse meat, including fish; moreover, they will not slaughter their cows because cows are considered sacred. Muslims in India, Pakistan, and Bangladesh refuse to eat pork even under desperate circumstances. Among some African tribes, children are discouraged from eating eggs. Relief workers in Nigeria discovered that Nigerian children would not eat if their parents were not present. In Bihar during 1966-1967, relief workers found that some famine victims preferred to risk starvation rather than consume millet rations. Many Asian people will not eat cheese and cannot tolerate milk.

Despite good intentions, donors have provided stricken communities with both useless and unfamiliar relief supplies. Following the Peruvian earthquake of 1970, relief agencies sent in vacation-type tents which blew away in the winds, and helicopters delivered powdered milk to Peruvian Indians whose crops were not affected by the quake and who did not normally drink cows milk. During the course of the 1968-1970 famine in Biafra, piles of unsorted clothing arrived for distribution by relief workers who could not obtain either vehicles or fuel to deliver them. Some relief foods, such as pickled vegetables and custard powder, were unsuitable for distribution. In the wake of a cyclone in 1974, a private relief agency gave priority to a shipment of woolen blankets to Bangladesh, when the people really needed clothing suitable for tropical weather. Some of the most bizarre relief donations were sent Cambodia in 1979-1980. William Shawcross reported that plane-loads of outdated drugs were sent to Cambodian refugees by a small American agency that had also sent waterbeds to Vietnamese boat people in Malaysia. A Japanese organization chartered a boat, at a cost of 500,000 dollars, and sent 500 Japanese youngsters to Thailand to spend four days teaching Cambodian refugee children how to play the harmonica. The American branch of La Leche League offered to send a plane-load of lactating mothers to suckle abandoned Khmer babies. Other agencies offered woolen blankets and foam rubber mattresses to refugees living in wet, humid tropics.

Medical intervention on behalf of famine victims has posed problems for both relief workers and their patients. Too often, volunteer personnel lack experience in famine relief work. Their assignments to famine zones last only a few weeks or months, and they do not have an opportunity to pass-on what they learned to successors. Worse yet, emergency medical intervention has often failed to incorporate measures designed to help famine victims after they return home. Records compiled by various relief teams in Biafra during 1967-1968 revealed that vitamin A deficiencies were common and that undernutrition had been rising even before the famine began. Within a short time, the incidence of kwashiorkor and marasmus reached "epidemic proportions." Famine refugees suffered from anemia, malaria, tuberculosis, diarrhea, and dehydration. Fifty to seventy percent of reported measles cases among children resulted in death. Inadequate transport made it difficult to provide either medicines or vaccines. Lack of funds made it impossible to provide nutritional rehabilitation which could be carried out after treatment for starvation. There were no measures designed to prevent continuing physical deterioration among famine refugees who returned home.

Drought conditions in the Sahel seemed to be over by spring 1975, and hunger no longer made headlines; however, people who returned to their homes suffered from beriberi, scurvy, tuberculosis, and viral hepatitis. Children continued to die from measles, whooping cough, and marasmus. No continuing relief measures were carried out on their behalf. In 1984-1985, Mali was spared the extreme famine which occurred in Ethiopia and, consequently, did not receive the attention or assistance that was directed to Ethiopian famine victims. However, fully 50% of the Mali children who contracted measles in 1985 died. The survivors often developed kwashiorkor. Youngsters were encouraged to eat insects as a source of protein and small boys sold rats at roadsides. No massive inoculation programs were undertaken.

It is generally agreed that one of the prime causes of famine in pre-industrial societies was the inability or unwillingness of officials and merchants to shift food surpluses from one region to another. Transportation difficulties still plague famine relief efforts. During one period in 1983, 40% of the trucks transporting water into drought-stricken northern India were out of commission. Relief workers in Mauritania during 1974 reported that it took six weeks for food supplies to reach the country and that, when they finally arrived, they rotted on the docks because it took another five weeks to move them from the ports to inland destinations. Airlifts were suggested, but it took one ton of fuel to move one ton of grain and there were no funds for such high transport costs. Lack of storage, transportation, manpower, and money delayed relief food shipments designated for an estimated ten million people in Nigeria in 1972. Both civil war and woefully inadequate transportation prevented donated food from reaching famine victims in Ethiopia, Sudan, and Chad during 1985. As a result, food distribution in many areas was well below the minimum needs of many victims.

The notion that women and children should be the primary targets of direct relief is widely accepted, because they are known to be the most vulnerable to the effects of famine. However some scholars have questioned the the wisdom of this practice. In his study of the 1943 famine in Bengal, Paul Greenough explained the evolution of the "Birkenhead rule" which dictates that women and children should be given the first opportunity to survive any crisis.

When the British naval vessel HMS *Birkenhead* sank off the coast of Africa in 1852, 450 people—mostly men—drowned while women and children boarded the two serviceable lifeboats. Greenough observed that the protective male attitude toward the weak and defenseless during a crisis was an inherent part of Victorian civilization and that it is still active in Euro-American culture. While he did not challenge the studies which demonstrate that women and children are more vulnerable to starvation than able-bodied men, he did question the wisdom of distributing famine relief according to the weakest victims while neglecting the able-bodied who are the most helpful in ending the crisis.

One example of an attempt to give relief priority to able-bodied men occurred under American Red Cross auspices in China during 1921-1922. Red Cross agents provided aid in the form of work-relief to able-bodied men. They made their decision on the assumption that recipients would, in turn, provide for their families. The Red Cross Report explained:

> Believing that at the best, we should fall short of preventing an appalling loss of life, it became necessary to consider who—what classes—should be saved. The classes most useful to the province would be the choice of any sociologist.

Members of missionary groups in China during the same period adopted methods similar to present-day approaches by caring first for the neediest and most helpless members of famine-stricken communities and by allowing the able-bodied to survive on their own resources. The decision was not an easy one. A later report explained:

> This...group comprised the backbone of the country life, and were the ones who, if helped, would be of the greatest good to the country. Humanitarian grounds compelled the passing by of this group and the giving of relief to those completely destitute, even though they might be of less value to the community.

Questions regarding who shall be fed first are seldom raised in light of the emotions aroused by portraits of starving infants and their mothers. Popular responses to emotional images and appeals, however, might well be tempered by the long-term value of directing intensive aid toward those responsible for renewing food production and earning wages in the wake of famine. The moral and philosophical questions, and their final resolution, have not been a significant part of relief appeals or donor concerns during recent years. Exceptions have occurred in the case of work-relief projects, which fall in the domain of indirect relief.[3]

INDIRECT RELIEF: THEORY & PRACTICE

Indirect famine relief measures should be determined by local needs and timing. Their ineffectiveness in the past has resulted from defective planning, underestimation of the physical capacities of famine victims, and inadequate funding. Tax reductions or remissions have released funds for immediate food purchases, but have seldom helped to avert permanent impoverishment among famine survivors. Grants of seeds, animals, and tools cannot be utilized until a famine zone and its population are on the verge of returning to a pre-famine condition. Public works projects have a mixed record. They tend to favor able-bodied individuals who possess the physical strength needed to move to where work is available. Wages in the form of cash or food may not be divided equally among the neediest members of famine-stricken communities. Political and community leaders often fail to agree upon what projects are needed or when they should be undertaken. As a result, any number of work relief projects have proven useless in communities where they were carried out, and many more have never been instituted.

A long-standing problem for relief agencies has been to sustain donor interest in the ongoing problems of famine victims so that relief funds could be devoted to programs which incorporated both direct and indirect relief projects. In some cases, health improvements achieved in famine refugee camps have been remarkable, but no provisions were made to improve dietary and medical conditions once acute famine conditions ended. In other cases, the social disorganization which characterizes famines could have been reversed more quickly if relief agencies had been able to reunite families, return them to their homes, and assist them in renewing agricultural production and cottage industries.

Indirect relief has great potential, but it has not proven successful in recent years. For example, the people of Bihar,

India, suffer from chronic undernutrition, anemia, parasites, and tuberculosis during ordinary times. When famine was declared in 1966, physical disorders, which Ramalingaswami and colleagues called the "unmasking of a colossal problem of chronic malnutrition in a population with no nutritional reserves," rendered most of the population too weak to do hard physical labor. Furthermore, the deterioration of roads during the 1967 monsoon made it impossible for even the able-bodied to reach work-relief projects. As a result, plans for several work-relief projects had to be abandoned. In Cambodia, refugees received massive food shipments from foreign donors in 1980-1981, but the same donors would not pay for repairs of irrigation systems, power stations, or transport systems.

LONG-TERM RELIEF
    The issues surrounding long-term famine intervention, rehabilitation, and prevention remain among the most difficult to resolve. When technological innovations have been inappropriate to affected areas, when they have been ill-designed to fill the particular needs of the areas, and when they have lacked skilled supervision and adequate funding, they have failed. Long-term projects have also failed when they lacked programs for training members of famine-stricken communities to supervise and maintain them after famine conditions have subsided. Additional failures have resulted when long-term projects have ignored the needs and desires of the existing political, economic and social orders. Programs set forth by individuals or organizations lacking field experience have met with failure because they ignored local needs as well as the need for local materials, expertise, and cooperation.[4]

GENERAL RELIEF DISORDERS
    The following examples are drawn from case studies which illustrate some of the ways in which famine relief measures have been diminished, delayed, misguided, or influenced by donors' political positions and objectives. Most of all, they illustrate some of the complex problems involved in providing for famine victims. In Bangladesh, a cyclone in 1970, a war in 1971, a stagnant economy, dependence upon rice as the major food crop, and high

mortality rates from severe malnutrition and infectious diseases during ordinary times helped to set the stage for famine conditions. In 1974, unseasonal flooding caused an estimated seventy thousand deaths from drowning. Nearly half the nation was inundated. Food crops and food stores were destroyed. Although some rice was still available, the vast majority of people did not have enough money to buy it. Hoarding and a black market drove prices to more than fifty cents a pound in a area with an annual per capita income of only seventy dollars a year. The prices of other foods rose from two hundred to five hundred percent. The government of Bangladesh received emergency grain shipments from North America, Australia, Europe and India, but so much was siphoned off by corrupt officials that famine victims received only a fraction of what was made available. Although some one hundred private organizations attempted to provide additional assistance to supplement foreign government shipments, Jean Mayer observed that international aid to Bangladesh actually was hampered by the fact that more than one government was involved, because each was attempting to protect or further its own interests by providing aid. After viewing the human tragedy that characterized famine conditions in Bangladesh, photo-journalist Steve Raymer wrote:

> I see a child—a naked skeleton—waiting for his meager ration; his withered body bears the telltale signs of advanced malnutrition. Others like him sit almost lifeless in their filth. A woman clad in rags clutches an infant so thin his ribs look like a birdcage beneath his peeling skin. I see a tear in the mother's eye.

In 1983, tens of thousands of people starved in Mozambique during the course of what Joseph Hanlon called an "entirely man made famine." Donors did not respond until foreign diplomats visited famine zones, saw conditions for themselves, and agreed to transmit appeals for aid. However, none of them would act until the United States signaled that aid was acceptable. By then, the worst was over.

An Example of Successful Measures

Despite the failures of indirect work-relief projects in Bihar during 1966-1967, which were noted above, and in spite of delays in recognizing acute food deficit, the Indian government ultimately did a notable job of averting widespread starvation. When famine conditions were recognized, voluntary agencies were already at work in other states and were prepared to undertake relief work in Bihar. Transport and storage facilities in Bihar were adequate and port capacity already had been streamlined. Most important, the government prepared, published, and distributed a Famine Code to serve as a standard guide to relief operations.

In accordance with the Code, relief operations took form in food distributions made through some twenty-thousand "fair price shops" at fixed, subsidized prices. An estimated one and one-half million tons of grain were distributed to almost 47 million people in 1967 alone. Free kitchens were run by local volunteer agencies. Relief works were carried out with an emphasis on long-term famine prevention measures, and wage policies were flexible enough to permit payments in both food and money. Good communications and the use of local administrators helped to simplify bureaucratic procedures and promote energetic coordination. Recognition that chronic malnutrition contributed to high death rates prompted the Central Food Technology Institute in Mysore to formulate a cereal-based high protein food called *Bal-Ahar* (Hindi for "Child's Food") which consisted of imported American grain with peanut meal, vitamins, and minerals added. Inoculations against small pox and cholera and careful disinfection of wells reduced death rates from infectious diseases. A review of relief records later revealed that, in many cases, health conditions among children actually improved. They had more milk in 1967 than ever before, they were given more than one ton of nutritional iron to combat chronic anemia, and vitamin, mineral, and protein supplements were made available.

Evaluation of Famine Relief

In many cases, recent famine relief operations have achieved the goal of saving lives threatened by starvation and epidemic disease. In a few, they have helped restore famine-stricken communities to normal activities. Unfortunately, examples of ill-conceived relief, which range from careless to bizarre, have demonstrated that theoretical approaches to effective famine relief have not been applied evenly or equally in all situations. Furthermore, any number of relief operations have been unsuccessful because of poor management, inadequate cooperation, or failure to monitor aid collections and distributions. Prospects for improvement have been diminished because evidence of errors in relief planning and institution has seldom been used to exert influence for significant change. Large aid organizations rarely carry out major reviews of their operations and, when they do, the results are not necessarily made public. Morris Davis wrote:

> Publications issued by relief agencies are generally designed to enhance their reputations and thereby both to satisfy past sources of funding and to elicit support in the future. These self-portraits also usually reflect home office syntheses rather than massings of observations by men in the field.

A paramount task in organizing and providing famine relief has been that of arranging cooperation among local, national and international representatives of both voluntary and government relief organizations. The need for multilateral cooperation has been accompanied by the need to recognize that famine relief has been, and probably will continue to be, helped or hindered by humanitarian motivation and by political will among both donor and recipient nations. [5]

RECOMMENDATIONS FOR IMPROVEMENTS

Many famine relief experts support the argument that, when famine intervention consists only of short-term food relief designed to halt starvation, or of emergency measures to control epidemic diseases, survivors remain weakened physically and crippled economically. They lack the means to improve upon marginal subsistence patterns which produce vulnerability to starvation and accelerate the decline to famine, and they become the first victims of any repeated episode of acute food deficit. Emergency feeding should be undertaken as the first among many measures designed to eliminate the causes of famine.

Relief experts now perceive their task as one of convincing individuals and organizations that support for famine relief operations includes the need to contribute to long-term famine prevention measures that will extend beyond the time, material, personnel, and funding required to carry out short-term emergency measures. A consensus among present-day experts further holds that long-term famine relief programs should include measures to prevent recurrent famines by using established rather than emergency organizations to channel resources into stricken areas, by expanding upon traditional relief and rehabilitation measures, and by using indigenous leaders to help introduce and promulgate new measures. Monitoring the nutritional and parasitic disorders associated with chronic hunger, and establishing local facilities to treat them, could have profound effects upon the goal of increasing individual and community productivity and thereby reducing vulnerability to starvation. Famine prevention measures should encompass development schemes designed to improve food production and distribution through new methods in animal husbandry, the increased use of irrigation and fertilizer, and assistance with the development and dissemination of new seeds for major crops. Above all, indirect and long-term relief projects should be designed to help hungry people to feed themselves.

Some relief experts have recommended the establishment of famine warning systems designed to monitor food production, distribution and consumption, as well as to provide information on impending shortages, so that aid can be mobilized in advance of an acute food deficit. Others have advocated the establishment of food banks designed to provide long-term insurance against crop failures. If such systems and facilities were functioning, transport and communications could be organized to permit food surpluses to reach threatened areas in time to avert starvation. To that end, a number of food relief experts have called for the establishment of a permanent body to coordinate and direct all phases of preventing or arresting acute food deficit, for global monitoring of food resources, and for international cooperation in accelerating food shipments to deficit regions in advance of the decline to actual famine conditions. Many of them have also suggested the establishment of training programs designed to prepare individuals from many disciplines in ways to cope with famine conditions, and they have asked for the publication of a manual for relief workers which would set forth universal principles for carrying our relief operations and provide a way of communicating the details of different experiences among relief workers in many parts of the world. [6]

SUMMARY

It is a tragedy of the times in which we live that success in carrying out programs for famine relief and prevention cannot be recorded for more than a few isolated cases. The lessons of the past do not seem to have provided solutions for the present. Present-day relief experts bemoan the constant repetition of ad hoc measures, the fact that relief agencies have demonstrated so little interest in sponsoring training programs for relief workers, and the general ineffectiveness of communication about the physiological, psychological and sociological problems associated with famine. Their sense of discouragement is not new. Dr. William Stokes wrote in the wake of famine in Ireland in the 1840s:

> If many were lost, perhaps ignorantly, let us think on the number saved. We cannot suddenly be wise. Nations, as well as individuals, must purchase experience, even though it can be ruinous....

The fact that nations have not been successful in efforts to "purchase experience" was made clear in the sentiment expressed by Gould regarding famine conditions which occurred in the Sahel more than one hundred years later:

> When the next crisis comes, little will have been learnt, the great relief efforts will start all over again from scratch, and everyone will be surprised at the 'sudden' arrival of a new famine in the Sahel, the Punjab,...who knows where? [7]

Notes

1. Direct, indirect and long-term relief measures are explained, and ideas for organizing and improving upon them are set forth in Mayer [324, 326], Miller & Holt [399], Cuny [338, 355], Garcia and Garcia & Escudero [300, 301], Den Hartog [308], Kapsiotis [322], and Masefield [292].

2. Food and medical relief are explained in several of the entries in Blix [316]. See especially Berg [336], Benoga [337], Ifekwunigwe [341], Masefield [343], and Monckeberg [346]. In Robson [294], see Bang [335], Cuny [338], Hay [340] and Manetsch [342]. de Ville de Goyet [350] is devoted solely to emergency intervention; Apeldoorn [414] and Chen [545] offer case studies.

3. Problems in providing direct relief are discussed by Benoga [337], Miller & Holt [399], and Tepley [349]. McCance [291] discusses allergies and aversions in general. Specific examples are in Mariam [297], Simoons [313, 314], Aall [334], and Mayer [370]. Examples of inappropriate provision of relief foods and supplies discussed in the text are in Taylor & Cuny [364], Aall [334], Mayer [370] Shawcross [450], Foege [283], Apeldoorn [414], Sheets & Morris [331], and Bullock [252]. The role of cultural attitudes in providing relief is discussed in Greenough [302], American Red Cross [466], and Peking United International Famine Relief Commission [476]. Greenough observed that it is not possible to predict patterns of mortality as long as cultural interventions prevent physiological processes from determining survival. American Red Cross work relief programs were not repeated in China. The China International Famine Relief Commission [470], see Nathan [474], attempted to follow Red Cross patterns, but emergency needs and short funding made it impossible to do so. [See Chapter V on China, 1921-1922].

4. Discussions on the problems of indirect and long-term famine relief are in Franke & Chasin [423], Cuny [355], Mayer [324], Gwatkin and colleagues [190], Sterling [429], and United States Agency for International Development [592]. Specific examples of problems are in Ramalingaswami and colleagues [542] and Shawcross [450].

5. Failures and successes among relief operations are explained in Chen [545], Chen & Rohde [546] and Raymer [550] for Bangladesh, in Hanlon [413] for Mozambique, and in Berg [336], Halse [541], and Ramalingaswami and colleagues [542] for Bihar. Among the many references to Ethiopia, see Davis [367], Passmore [328], Green [357], and May [344, 345]. In addition, see Passmore [328] and Davis [367] on the problems of providing relief amidst hostilities and on difficulties in evaluating relief efforts.

6. Recommendations for famine prevention have been set forth in numerous studies. A few of them are in Kapsiotis [322], Pirie [329], Latham [290], Dando [288], Mayer [324], Nicol [293], and Gould [425].

7. Citations in the summary remarks are from MacArthur (quoting Stokes) [284] and Gould [425].

IV

Nineteenth Century Famines

Some of the famines which occurred during the nineteenth century are examined in this chapter. The primary focus is upon the ways in which different governments approached the problems associated with famine conditions. The first areas discussed, Ireland and India, were under British rule. The second area, China, found both Chinese and foreign measures for famine intervention being carried out during the latter part of the nineteenth century. The third and fourth areas examined are Europe and Russia, after the Napoleonic Wars, when famine conditions were met by a growing state responsibility for public welfare during periods of acute food deficit. In each case, famine intervention attitudes and approaches that evolved before and during the nineteenth century influenced methods employed during the twentieth century.

IRELAND, 1846-1848

According to traditional British policies, famine intervention was based upon a laissez-faire theory of economics, a belief that charity was degrading to its recipients, and a faith in the value of public works. Famine was not perceived as the result of absolute grain shortage, but as a consequence of high food prices combined with unemployment. Therefore, remedies took form in two stages. The first was to permit complete freedom of grain trade so that foodstuffs would flow naturally into the areas of greatest demand and highest prices. The second was to provide work for famine victims so that they could use earnings to buy food.

The Irish famine of 1846-1848 is remembered as the most outstanding example of widespread starvation precipitated by a plant disease. The potato probably was introduced into Ireland early in the seventeenth century. Within less than one hundred years, it accounted for about 80% of food intake among the Irish people. Cabbage and milk were the major supplements. As a staple food, supplemented by dairy products and some vegetables, the potato provided adequate sustenance. In addition, it could be fed to cattle, pigs, and chickens. However, dependence upon the potato left no way to maintain a food reserve. Potatoes did not store well from season to season and, when supplies ran out, there was no cheap food to use as a last resort and no replacement crop. Grain crops, such as wheat and oats, were grown by farmers as a means to pay rents and were not used for direct consumption.

The famine which Cecil Woodham-Smith called "the great hunger" was not an unusual event for its time. Other major famines had occurred in 1739, 1800, and 1816. Nor was it a sudden event. It began in 1843, when localized crop failures caused severe want in some areas. Further crop failures occurred in 1844 and 1845. Then, in 1846, potato fields throughout the country were covered with luxuriant growth one day and, on the next, turned into what Gallagher called "a blackened mass of corruption."

The potato blight was caused by the fungus *Phytophthora infestans,* a microscopic organism which attacked plants along the Atlantic coast in America and Canada in 1842, and which probably was transmitted to Europe in diseased tubers. Potato crops also failed in France, Belgium, Holland, Germany, and Russia but, in those countries, food exports were halted and food imports and transfers were accelerated. Hardship existed, but not famine. In Ireland, a majority of the people were deprived of their major food source as soon as the potato crop failed; however, no official action was taken to avert widespread starvation by providing alternate food supplies.

People subsisted on turnips while they were available; many drank blood from their cattle or killed and ate them because the animals were also starving. In coastal regions, they ate seaweed with sometimes fatal results because nobody knew which varieties were safe and which were not. Seeds, sheep, and horses were consumed rapidly. Then people ate dogs, rats, and dead humans. Tenants who could not pay their rents were expelled from the land and began to migrate toward large towns and cities in search of work and food. People committed petty crimes in the hope of being sent to jail where they would be fed. Thousands died of typhus and dysentery. Scurvy did not occur in Ireland during ordinary times because of the high vitamin C content in potatoes. During the famine years, however, it was widespread. Victims had spongy gums, their teeth fell out, their joints became swollen and painful, and blood vessels which burst under their skin produced dark blotches which, in the Irish colloquial language, were called "black leg." Sir William MacArthur, a physician, described famine victims:

> Large numbers had some variety of fever along with dysentery, and often scurvy or famine dropsy as well, and so did not die of one disease but from a combination of causes....

The British government refused to halt food exports from Ireland. Wheat and oats were transported to England instead of being retained to replace losses caused by potato crop failures. When some action finally was considered, in November 1845, it was to form local committees to raise funds and buy food for resale or as payment for small-scale work projects on local estates. Other measures were designed to create extra employment by building new roads and by establishing workhouses to care for the destitute and to provide them with a gainful occupation. Some road construction projects were organized, but famine victims often had to walk miles to reach them and many died on their way. Workhouses were inadequate to the growing demand for jobs, food, shelter, and medical care. To make matters worse, relief of any kind was limited to people who were destitute because of the potato. It was an impossible situation. As Woodham-Smith explained:

> Disaster was the normal condition of a great mass of the Irish people, and the Poor Inquiry Commission had stated that 2,385,500 persons

were in a state of semi-starvation every year, whether the potato failed or not.

Corn imports were arranged from America in order to keep food prices down by filling markets, and English ports were opened to receive shipments. However, supplies were restricted because sailing ships could not cross the Atlantic during late autumn and winter, and because the 1845 crop already had been sold to other European countries. Orders that were transmitted in September 1845 could not be filled before the spring of 1846. Furthermore, the British ordered Indian corn or "flint corn" which also was known as "hominy." In order to process it for consumption, it had to be chopped in steel mills; ordinary mill stones required a double operation and gave poor results. Unfortunately, there were no steel mills in Ireland and very few people had mill stones. Therefore, the corn could only be soaked and boiled to make it fit for consumption. People who did not have the utensils needed for soaking, or the fuel for boiling, had to eat the corn dry. As a result, thousands suffered from intestinal irritations and diarrhea, and hundreds died from gangrene of the intestines. The Irish people began to call the relief corn "Peel's brimstone" after Prime Minister Robert Peel who had ordered it.

In 1847, when the world finally learned about famine conditions in Ireland and began sending private relief donations for the Irish people, the British government allowed relief ships to go directly to Ireland rather than have their cargoes transferred to British vessels and submit to added freight charges as had been the practice. Another result of outside criticism of British relief policies was the passage of a Poor Relief Bill that advanced ten million pounds for relief work in Ireland. One-half of the sum was to be spent on public works, and the other half was to be used to establish outdoor soup kitchens. The soup kitchens became a source of bitter humor. Alexis Soyer, chef de cuisine at the Reform Club of London, was assigned the task of concocting recipes for relief soup. An article in the British medical publication, *The Lancet,* called Soyer's mixtures a "quackery" that was taken up by the rich as "a salve for their consciences."

During ordinary times, the Irish regarded leaving their home land a terrible fate. During the famine years, however, more than one million of them left their country for North America and parts of Great Britain. About 70,000 died enroute to their destinations. According to various estimates, Ireland's population declined some two to three million between 1846 and 1848 as a result of starvation, disease, and migration.

British government measures on behalf of Irish relief were ill-conceived and inadequate. Halting food exports and opening relief operations earlier, with more thought to victims' needs, might have reduced the death toll. Rapid intervention by central authorities could have facilitated wide-scale relief operations. Funds allocated for public works were devoted to projects which had nothing to do with rehabilitating agriculture, improving the public transportation system, or otherwise enhancing Ireland's physical infrastructure. On the other hand, it must be remembered that official and popular attitudes toward relief were characteristic of the period. Most relief schemes were carried out by local authorities without central direction or assistance. The laissez-faire attitude toward economics did not make allowances for interference with market forces or with the flow of goods. It should also be noted that, by summer 1847, a new Whig government did help to feed some three million people in Ireland. Eventually, British failures in Ireland helped to restructure famine intervention methods in India and to accelerate acceptance of the idea that the government had a responsibility for saving lives during periods of famine.[1]

INDIA, 1769-1900

Recurrent episodes of famine in India took an enormous toll of human life from the mid-eighteenth century to the beginning of the twentieth. An estimated 10 million people died of starvation and disease during the 1769-1770 famine in Bengal. East India Company officials refused to institute relief measures that might have interfered with trade activities, but public outcry in England led to passage of the Regulating Act of 1773. The Act was designed to improve administration in India, but it did not include famine relief measures. During the Madras famine of 1781-1783, officials attempted to remit import duties on grain and to fix prices on grain sales, but they had to relax their regulations in order to accommodate the demands of the trading community. Thus, the response to famine in Madras was marked by the first official attempt to fix grain prices during a period of famine, but no positive relief measures were undertaken.

The years 1800-1825 were marked by increasing British governmental control, by a growing alienation of the common people from the government, and by recurrent episodes of famine. Rents rose, farmers were forced to surrender surplus food during good years so that they had no reserves against crop failures and, when food was in short supply, grain traders raised their prices. The British government did little in the way of direct relief and did not consider long-term preventive measures. The only consistent official policy was faith in free trade and, when disaster struck, response took the form of ad hoc measures directed toward work relief.

Wallace Aykroyd described response to famine in India in 1812 as a classic example of relief denied because of British government policy:

> Adam Smith's book, *The Wealth of Nations,* influenced famine relief in India as in Ireland. In 1812 the Government of Bombay, faced with an episode of food shortage...refused to interfere in any way with private trade. The Governor recorded in a special minute his adherence to the principles of political economy....Another dogma which affected governmental action against famine was that giving anything away for nothing...demoralized the recipients and led to "pauperism".

Two themes emerged from British experiences with work relief programs. The first was a belief that no relief should be given without work in return. The second was the view that relief should not be given in the form of grain so that distributions would not interfere with the free working of the grain market. Despite policies to the contrary, the Madras government did open food kitchens for people who were unable to work and, for the first time, established hospitals for famine victims. The small changes were not part of a trend. Alamgir noted that, according to famine accounts from the period, "the government always failed to recognize the severity of the calamity in time, and, on occasion, it refused to acknowledge the phenomenon even when it was at the doorstep."

The first famine after the introduction of direct British rule in India occurred in the northwest provinces and the Punjab in 1860. Some of the positive measures which had been attempted in Ireland in the 1840s were repeated and, for the first time, the government made advances to farmers so that they could buy seeds and animals to renew agricultural production. However, there was no real departure from free-trade doctrines and Great Britain already had begun to export grain from India. Internal food prices began a steady rise while wages remained stationary and population growth contributed to unemployment.

Lack of rainfall precipitated famine conditions in Orissa, and in parts of Bengal, Bihar, and Madras in 1865. Despite warnings from local officials that measures should be taken to avert starvation by importing food, grain exports were continued. The government did not have any set procedures for coping with extreme food shortages. Local measures included opening kitchens in small towns and distributing cash and grain to the needy in exchange for labor on relief works. Although central relief efforts were negligible, the government of India appointed a commission to investigate the causes of the 1866 famine and to suggest remedial measures. The Commission recommended that the government consider liberal assessments of land revenue, removal of intermediaries from the land, strengthening land occupancy rights, improving the terms of existing settlements, expanding railways and roads, and improving irrigation systems. However, the Commission did not recommend controlling food-grain exports, deviating from free-trade principles, or changing official methods for famine intervention.

During and after the 1866-1868 famine, a major government concern was the cost of famine relief. It had been expressed in an earlier dispatch to the Secretary of State:

> While the necessity of preventing, as far as practicable, death by starvation is paramount, the financial embarrassment which must in any case arise, will be most difficult to overcome, and any departure from the most rigid economy, or from the principles in dealing with famine which experience has confirmed as sound, only aggravate it to a degree which cannot be estimated.

Famine conditions in 1876-1878, 1896-1897, and 1899-1900 claimed more than five million lives. Each time, the effects of harvest failures were compounded by pre-existing economic difficulties associated with high taxes, high rents, and high interest payments demanded by government, landlords, and moneylenders.

The monsoon failed in southern India in 1876, and in the north in 1877. In Madras alone, an estimated 3.5 million people died of starvation, "alvine fluxes" (diarrhea and dysentery), cholera, smallpox, and pneumonia. Local officials debated making grain purchases, but the government of India rejected the idea by insisting that such purchases would constitute government intervention in the market. Initially, the central authorities favored small work relief projects and compelled the government of Madras to accept their policy by limiting the amount of funds available for each project. Later, the Indian government reversed its stand and permitted the organization of larger projects. However, plans for public works produced wage controversies. The Madras government paid adult male laborers 1.5 pounds of grain per day, but Sir Richard Temple thought that the amount would encourage more people to seek work than was justified by their actual need. At his insistence, the ration was reduced to one pound per day. The new rate saved money for the government, but the cost in human lives and mounting pressure from England forced the government of India to relent and increase the ration.

The inadequacies of official relief during 1876-1878 prompted efforts to improve famine administration. In 1880, a Famine Commission prepared a Famine Code containing detailed instructions for all kinds of relief administration. The Commission argued that the state was responsible for famine relief and suggested measures which included large public works of "permanent utility," village relief, distribution of cooked food to the disabled, remission and suspension of revenue collections, and loans for seeds and cattle. However, because of continuing reliance upon free trade philosophies, neither the Commission nor the government of India saw any need to establish emergency food stores, to adopt measures for reducing chronic unemployment, or to address questions of famine prevention. The most important outcome of the Famine Commission's efforts was the consolidation of existing measures into a Famine Code which could be used as a model for provincial governments.

Crop failures in Bengal during 1896-1897 caused grain prices to triple between April and August 1897. In accordance with the Famine Code, official work relief projects were begun by autumn and free relief in the form of money or food was provided for children, for women who could not work, and for the elderly. Unfortunately, the tragedies of earlier famines were repeated because central authorities would not permit provincial governments to interfere in the grain market in order to reduce food prices.

Whether or not British conduct was entirely to blame for a rise in the number of famines in India during the eighteenth and nineteenth centuries has been a subject of scholarly debate. Rhomesh Dutt blamed British rule for the increasing frequency of famines; Ambirajan called laissez faire "a God that failed." B.M. Bhatia wrote that the reason for increases in famine conditions lay in growing vulnerability to starvation among agricultural laborers, weavers, and tenant cultivators during an era when tax burdens fell heaviest upon the poor. Srivastava did not hesitate to criticize British rule, but he argued that recurrent episodes of famine ultimately encouraged positive change because they:

> ...obliged the Government to develop agriculture, extend irrigation, railways and other means of communications, enact laws to regulate advances and credit facilities, initiate agricultural education and research, establish Co-operative Societies, introduce land reforms and attempt many other measures of a similar natur

He also pointed to the fact that changes in India's infrastructure did not derive from concern with popular welfare, but from the effects of popular pressure.

> It is doubtful if the Government would have undertaken any of these measures if it had not been faced by public criticism and exposure of its policy by the Famine Commissions.

Srivastava criticized the government for failing to undertake famine relief measures promptly or vigorously, but gave it credit for the efforts which it made.

> Basic measures to check famines were never attempted with any real
> vigour or perspicacity. A true famine policy...should have been a
> gigantic effort to prevent pauperism....Due credit must nevertheless
> be given to the alien ruler for having organized, codified and sowed
> the seeds of a correct famine relief policy. What was actually
> accomplished was more than what any other previous Government in
> India had done in the matter of both relief and protection.

British policies have been defended on the grounds that
transportation, rather than official policy, was inadequate. The
Report of the Famine Commission for 1901 emphasized the
problems associated with poor transportation facilities:

> ...relief was to a large extent insufficient, and to a large extent
> imperfectly organized; the insufficiency being largely due to the
> inability of private trade, hampered by want of railways and
> communication, to supply the demand for food.

Michelle McAlpin's study of famine in Western India from
1860 to 1920 also defended British government policies by
presenting data which revealed that subsistence levels during those
years actually improved for millions and that credit for the
improvements could be attributed to British rule. According to
McAlpin, land taxes fell in the western part of India after the
middle of the nineteenth century, the prices paid for food rose, and
the railways created an expanded market which helped to reduce
individual cultivators' dependence upon their own production.
Thus, weather played a greater role in precipitating famine than
government neglect, and neither economic gains nor improved
transport facilities could have helped to avert starvation.

British response to famine in India was the product of an era
characterized by government reluctance to interfere with trade and
commerce. While it may not be fair to judge nineteenth century
famine policies in Ireland and India according to present-day
attitudes, it is interesting to compare British policies with those
which had prevailed in China for centuries.[2]

CHINA, 1876-1900

Traditional Chinese methods for famine intervention were markedly different from those of the British government. As Lillian Li noted:

> From ancient times, the promotion of the welfare of the people was regarded as a major function of the Chinese state. The Chinese state saw itself presiding over an agrarian society, where its chief functions were to maintain harmony and ensure the livelihood of the people. To this end it sought to promote agricultural production and to see that people had the means by which they could till the land....The failure of the state to provide basic sustenance for the people was taken to be sign of its imminent decline....The dynasty endeavored to forestall its seemingly inevitable decline by using all means at its disposal to prevent such calamities.

Centuries of official concern with the causes and effects of famine gave rise to a diverse body of literature which described different episodes of famine and which listed a variety of direct, indirect, and long-term methods for dealing with famine conditions. Lists of historical events which precipitated famine conditions noted the differences between "heavenly calamities" such as flood and drought, and those which resulted from the interaction of natural and human forces such as rebellion and war. A guiding principle for famine intervention held that relief efforts had to be tailored to each episode, because the causes and effects of famine were not always the same. The decline to famine was described in terms of degrees of hunger, or according to the amount of food which was available per person during a given period.

Relief measures were implemented by local officials who investigated and reported on physical losses, popular distress, and prevalent needs. Direct relief measures included free distributions of food and cash designed to halt starvation. Indirect measures included tax reductions, deferments or remissions, seed distributions to help restore agricultural productivity, and work-relief projects designed to repair famine-related damage and prevent its recurrence. In many instances, projects were planned in advance of actual needs so that they could be implemented quickly and without controversy. Long-term relief measures included plans for major water conservancy projects and schemes for creating settlements on unused land. Grain storage facilities, commonly known as "ever-normal granaries," provided insurance against crop failures by permitting officials to stabilize grain prices and, when crops failed, to sell grain at reduced prices and to move grain from surplus areas to deficit areas.

Famine intervention had notable successes when China had a strong central administration, and equally notable failures when the state was weak. During famine periods in the 1590s, and again in the 1740s, official measures helped to provide relief for several million people for periods of about two years each time. However, by the middle of the nineteenth century, the effects of inadequate economic resources were worsened by social upheavals and widespread rebellions which diminished state and local resources needed to maintain a physical infrastructure of irrigation works, dike maintenance, and transportation essential to produce and exchange food supplies and to provide famine relief. As a result of declining central powers and diminishing administrative and physical resources, famines took enormous tolls during the nineteenth century, and recurrent famine conditions extended well into the twentieth.

The Great Northern Famine, 1876-1879
Crops failed for three years before famine was declared in northern China during 1876. Despite local and central government efforts to administer relief, the means available to arrest starvation were totally inadequate. Starvation and disease claimed 9 to 13 million lives between 1876 and 1879. Another million deaths occurred between 1892 and 1894 in the same general area and for the same reasons. The Chinese state could not mobilize either the administrative or the financial resources needed to carry out traditional famine relief measures. Recurrent episodes of famine, which continued into the twentieth century, were a paramount sign of the state's inability to fulfill traditional obligations on behalf of popular welfare during ordinary times, or to provide for relief and rehabilitation during critical times.

Foreign relief efforts in China began during the famine years of 1876-1879 when appeals from missionaries helped to focus international attention upon the plight of Chinese famine victims.

Their aid consisted primarily of distributing money to famine victims to enable them to buy food. Foreign relief work in China was hindered by differences among missionaries concerning their role as relief agents, by reticence among Chinese officials, and by hostility among members of the foreign business community in China's treaty ports. Some missionaries refused to participate in famine relief work, because they did not feel that it was a "proper spiritual concern." Others used relief distributions as an opportunity to distribute scriptural tracts and conduct religious services. Some missionaries supported the idea of instituting work relief projects, but they did not carry them out because they did not want to undertake projects which might have political implications. Any number of foreigners in China, including missionaries, insisted that the incidence of famine could be reduced by deepening canals, building railways, and otherwise encouraging trade. Chinese officials who rejected their ideas acknowledged the importance of making improvements in China's transportation systems, but asserted that similar improvements undertaken by the British in India had accelerated foreign military and economic penetration into the country with little improvement of popular welfare. Hostility within the foreign business community toward famine relief efforts in China derived from reports of official corruption and inability to meet prevalent needs as well as from Chinese official unwillingness to initiate technological improvements under foreign auspices.

Nineteenth century foreign efforts to relieve famine in China yielded three themes which were reiterated throughout the first half of the twentieth century by a variety of relief agents and agencies, by Chinese officials, and by foreign donors. The first was the idea that popular welfare could only be improved, and the incidence of famine reduced, by long-term physical and economic improvements. The second consisted of negative press reports which discouraged foreign donors from contributing to any measures beyond direct emergency relief. Third, Chinese officials continued to accept foreign food and money to support emergency measures, but they regularly rejected proposals which involved foreign supervision of long-term projects. As a result, while the British in India developed famine codes as a part of an assumed responsibility for famine intervention, foreign efforts in China did not evolve into coherent programs for direct, indirect, or long-term relief.[3]

EUROPE, 1816-1817

John D. Post's study, *The Last Great Subsistence Crisis in the Western World,* attributed famine conditions in Europe during 1816-1817 to crop failures resulting from a change in weather patterns caused by the explosion of Tomboro, a volcano located on Sumbawa, Indonesia. The meteorological effects produced by volcanic dust veils caused unseasonable cold in the Northern Hemisphere during the spring and summer of 1816. Crop failures occured in the eastern United States, Canada, Japan, and India. In Europe, food deficits compounded the effects of economic and social disruptions associated with the end of the Napoleonic wars. When food prices rose beyond the reach of ordinary wage earners, hunger and epidemic disease outbreaks ensued.

European governments adopted various measures to compensate for grain deficits. They included prohibiting grain exports and making arrangements for food imports from areas with surplus production. Both the United States and the Russian empire provided grain. As a result of state controls over grain movements and subsequent reductions in grain prices, famine conditions were mitigated in some parts of Europe. In others, there was a pervasive fear that they would not succeed. Food riots erupted in France, Belgium and Britain in 1816. In 1817, the pattern continued in Germany, Holland, Ireland, Switzerland, Italy and Norway. Thefts and crimes against property rose. Vagrants appeared in such numbers that 1817 was called "the year of the beggar" in central Europe.

Two different patterns of state intervention in relief measures emerged as food shortages increased and riots, crimes, and vagrancy continued. Governments in northwestern Europe and the Habsburg Monarchy authorized free internal grain trade, supplemented by imports; officials in the southwestern German states and the Swiss Cantons attempted to control every aspect of grain movement. In both cases, imported grain supplies were sold below market prices in rural areas in order to depress local prices. In urban areas, the same process was followed in order to assure that bakers would make bread available below normal market rates. Since bread was not enough to provide subsistence for unemployed workers, large-scale public works were undertaken to furnish employment. In France, they took form in road repairs. In the Netherlands, fortifications were built along the Franco-Belgian border. Officials in Swiss Cantons carried out land reclamation projects, men in the Rhineland were hired for various public works projects, and women were employed to knit clothing for the army. Roads and canals were constructed in Italy and in some areas under Habsburg control. The British government made some funds available for public works in 1817, but few were undertaken. Since work-relief projects could not help people who were unable to do heavy labor, soup kitchens were opened to provide free meals. Traditional appeals to private charities were continuous, and private funds played an important role in supplementing government sustenance for the poor.

None of the welfare programs carried out in 1816-1817 were particularly innovative, but official measures and welfare services were instituted on a more concentrated scale than during earlier periods, and relief mechanisms were enhanced by the government's importation and distribution of grain supplies. None of the affected countries were entirely dependent upon internal grain production for relief distributions.

While efforts to minimize deaths from starvation and disease were motivated in part by fear of popular disorder, they seem also to have reflected a heightened degree of humanitarian concern by government officials and the public at large. The greatest number of deaths from starvation and epidemic diseases were recorded in Italy, Switzerland, and the southern provinces of the Habsburg Monarchy. According to Post, higher death rates in those areas resulted more from high food prices and lack of government effectiveness in carrying out relief measures than from an absolute lack of food.[4]

RUSSIA, 1891-1892

Famine conditions occurred in Russia on an average of once every ten years between 971 and 1970 and, according to William Dando, they were more a product of human failures than of natural calamities. Dando wrote:

A Russian famine, historically, was a protracted shortage of total food over a large geographical region causing widespread disease and death from starvation. Gradual disappearance of food and food substitutes first produced emaciated, listless, weak individuals; then inactive, skeletonized, animal-like creatures sometimes waiting and many times hoping for death.

Systematic government relief activities began during the fifteenth century and increased following a series of bad harvests between 1721 and 1724. During those years, Tsar Peter I was compelled to respond with official measures which Richard Robbins termed "hastily improvised, unsystematic, and often draconian." They had few immediate or practical effects. However, some of the policies instituted during the 1720s did help to establish a tradition of direct state action in, and control over, famine relief.

By the nineteenth century, official measures took form in four general ways. First, grain storage, supplemented by public works and tax remissions, became the backbone of the state relief system. Second, the state abandoned the use of extreme measures such as the registration and requisition of grain or the reduction of official salaries in its struggles against famine. Third, legislation governing official intervention in grain trade was relaxed when the state recognized that it did not have the administrative machinery needed to implement stronger regulatory measures. Finally, Russian rulers sought to develop an effective method of supervising the empire's food supplies by decentralizing relief work. Local people, including state officials, nobles, and *zemstvos* (local self-governing councils), were assigned the tasks of gathering, maintaining, and distributing relief supplies, while the central government retained the power to supervise affairs and control finances.

Although Russian state measures seemed adequate in theory, they were not sufficient to avert the decline to famine among peasants whose liberation from serfdom had not been accompanied by improvements in agricultural techniques and whose surplus production was absorbed by a variety of direct and indirect taxes. Conditions in the agricultural sector were such that

the American Consul General at St. Petersburg predicted famine
conditions two years before they were declared:

> At present, the statesmen of Russia legislate for towns and cities
> principally. They seem oblivious of the millions of peasants on the
> brink of ruin; but some day there will be a rude awakening, and Tsar,
> Senate, Council, and Ministries will realize that the most industrious
> and loyal inhabitants of the Empire are no longer on the brink, but
> have absolutely fallen upon the charities of the country....

During the 1891-1892 famine, grain shipments were delayed
because transport facilities were inadequate. Relief schemes
which called for constructing church schools and grain elevators
were beneficial to skilled craftsmen, but they did not help
unskilled workers. Furthermore, the projects often were long
distances from workers' homes and, when cash distributions were
delayed, many workers had neither the food or the money
necessary for survival.

Richard Robbins has argued that despite the inadequacies of
state relief measures in 1891-1892 and the obstacles created by
prevalent unemployment, low wages, and high food prices, the
Russian government eventually mounted one of the largest relief
campaigns in its history. More than eleven million people received
official rations. While famine-related mortality has been estimated
at between 375,000 and 400,000, a significant number of the
deaths were due to cholera and typhus rather than to starvation.
According to Robbins, overall mortality was much lower than it
would have been without official intervention, and it was well
below the number of deaths that resulted from famines in China
and India during the same period. On the other hand, while
government intervention did help to reduce mortality rates, the
famine of 1890-1891 had a profound negative influence upon
intellectual perceptions of the existing regime and ultimately
influenced its demise.[5]

SUMMARY

The British economic system, based upon laissez-faire policies
and free trade doctrines, offered relatively little assistance to the
people of Ireland and India during their nineteenth century
famines. Public reaction to official policies did, however,

stimulate efforts to codify famine relief measures. The Codes which resulted were applied by the Indian government in Bihar during the twentieth century and the relief efforts which were carried out under their directions have been referred to by some present-day relief experts as a model upon which modern versions of universal methods for famine relief might be based. The Chinese traditional system for famine administration was based upon strong central controls over grain trade and distribution. When the state was powerful, it provided effective relief; when central controls were weak, famines took enormous tolls. Outside intervention in Ireland and India supplanted traditional relief systems by placing them under the control of the British government. Outside intervention in China enhanced traditional measures by providing food and funds which were distributed in the form of direct relief. European and Russian relief systems represented combinations of free trade and central control measures which were adjusted according to individual circumstances, and which succeeded or failed according to each state's capacity for social and economic intervention.

Notes

1. For a listing of sources specific to Ireland, see entries 552-563. Woodham-Smith [563] explained that the fungus which attacked Ireland's potato crop was not a sickness of the plants, but an invasion by a microscopic organism which was not understood in 1846, not recognized until 1861, and not treated until 1865. During the 1840s, scientists believed that the fungus was a consequence, not a cause, of decay.

2. In addition to comments by Aykroyd [524], see Bhatia [513], Alamgir [296], and Sen [305] for overviews of India's historic famine problems. See Patnaik [524] on famine in Orissa during the 1860s; Digby [518] and Porter (a medical account) [524] on famine conditions during the 1870s; and Carlyle [517] on the tasks assigned to British officials during the 1890s. Famine Codes are explained in Famine in India [591]. Assessments of British responses are in Ambirajan [516], Bhatia [513], and Srivastava [526, 527], among others. Rhomesh Dutt's thesis is criticized by McAlpin [515], who takes an opposing view.

3. For famine in pre-twentieth century China, see entries 455-464. Bohr [455] is the best English language source on famine during the 1870s. Hosie

[458, 459] and Yao [462, 463] provide data on climatic events. Li [453] and Hsiao [452] explain traditional Chinese official famine relief methods.

4. Post's study [509] is the most comprehensive examination of the causes and effects of famine in Europe, 1816-1817. The author provides insights into the effects of climatic change on agricultural production, examines official responses to crop failures throughout Europe, and discusses the incidence of starvation and epidemic diseases. Historic backgrounds on public conditions are in Blum [500] and Hufton [501].

5. Bibliographic entries 566-570 provide information on famine in Russia during the late nineteenth century. Historic background is outlined in Dando [566]. Hodgetts [567] provides a personal account. Comments by the American Consul General are cited in Queen [568]. Robbins [569] is the best general source on the famine of 1891-1892.

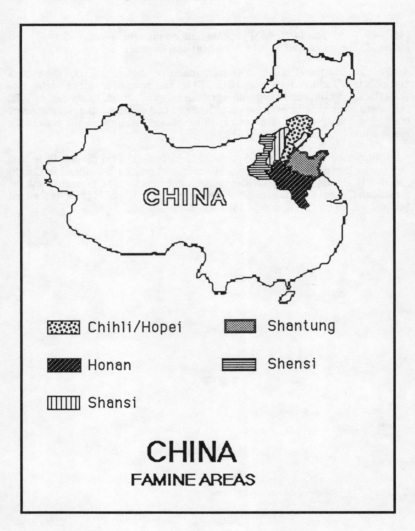

CHINA

Chihli/Hopei   Shantung

Honan   Shensi

Shansi

CHINA
FAMINE AREAS

V

Twentieth Century Famines, 1900-1949

This chapter examines famines which occurred in China and the Soviet Union during 1920-1922, and in China and in India during 1943-1944. There were strong continuities with the famine problems and the relief practices of the nineteenth century and, at the same time, there was evidence of new patterns of famine intervention emerging during and immediately after World War I and World War II. Neither the contents of this chapter nor the list of famines at the beginning of this study purport to examine more than a fraction of the enormous number of famines which occurred in different parts of the world during the half century under examination. If these famines were to be listed separately, they would appear as annual events.

CHINA, 1920-1921
    The decline of the Chinese government's capacity for famine intervention continued into the twentieth century. Major episodes of famine occurred in 1901-1902, 1906-1907, 1909-1912, 1920-1921, 1928-1930, 1931-1932, 1934-1935, and throughout the period from 1937-1949. The years 1900-1949 marked an era when food shortages and widespread endemic diseases rendered millions of Chinese vulnerable to starvation. They became the first victims of famine whenever their marginal subsistence was interrupted by drought, flood, rising food prices, civil unrest, or war.

Nineteenth century foreign relief efforts were carried forward into the twentieth century, but they did not evolve into coherent programs; they were not codified. Although some efforts were made to initiate measures for famine prevention, most foreign contributions were used to arrest starvation, and most foreign relief workers perceived famine intervention as a temporary activity. The famines of 1920-1921 and 1943-1944 provide examples of relatively successful and markedly unsuccessful interventions.

The military and political crises and the financial instability which characterized conditions in China during the early 1920s did not diminish foreign relief efforts. On the contrary, many foreigners, especially Americans who were living in China, sympathized with the new sense of nationalist pride that emerged in China after World War I. They hoped to take part in reducing widespread poverty through programs for rural education and agricultural improvement. In addition, members of the American diplomatic community hoped to mitigate the effects of Soviet overtures to the Chinese government in 1919.

Drought conditions caused poor harvests in 1919 and widespread crop failures in 1920 in China's northern provinces. Grain prices tripled in many areas, and some people began to starve because they could not afford available food supplies. In other areas, they starved within miles of railway stations piled high with grain because there were no means for transporting it into famine zones. By late summer 1920, sales of land, possessions, and even children, were accompanied by migrations in search of work and food. Missionaries were the first foreigners to report on conditions in the countryside, and they were the first to begin carrying out relief work. John Earl Baker, an American working as railway adviser to the Chinese Ministry of Communications, recognized that the region affected by drought was same area in which between nine and thirteen million people had died during the great famine of the 1870s. He transmitted his findings, along with missionary reports, to the American Minister in Peking. They agreed that immediate action was both necessary and appropriate.

Although there was a period of confusion regarding the implementation of relief measures, two major organized efforts, supplemented by numerous smaller ones, emerged. The first major effort was carried out independently by the American Red Cross. The second was organized under the auspices of a Sino-Western organization known as the Peking United International Famine Relief Committee (PUIFRC).

Red Cross relief took form in road-building projects which were supported by one million dollars drawn from its contingency funds. Red Cross agents could not overcome Chinese opposition to their initial plan to carry out a work relief project near the Grand Canal, because it would have interfered with relationships among Chinese political factions. The project which finally was approved represented a compromise with Chinese officials. It protected Chinese interests and, since the Red Cross did not appeal for popular donations in the United States, it did not risk offending donors whose goal in making relief contributions was to save starving Chinese and not to support public works projects.

Combined Chinese and foreign contributions to PUIFRC relief work exceeded 17 million dollars. Most of the funds donated by foreigners, about eight million dollars, were raised in the United States in response to appeals made by Presidents Wilson and Harding and collected by the American Committee for China Famine Fund under the leadership of Thomas Lamont. Relief agents in China requested direct transfers of money rather than food shipments. A good harvest in Manchuria and Chinese official control over existing railways made it cheaper to purchase food relatively close to famine zones, eliminated the need to await trans-Atlantic food shipments, and made it possible to avoid accepting inappropriate food donations. (Well-meaning Americans, for instance, had sent cheese to China during the 1906-1907 and 1911-1912 famines, but the Chinese would not eat it.) China's Railway Minister, Yeh Kung-cho, reduced freight charges by twenty-five percent on food shipments going into famine zones and increased them by the same amount on out-bound grain. The result was a flow of grain from areas with good crops into places which had none, an end to hoarding, and a drop in food prices.

While Red Cross operations were devoted solely to work-relief projects, most PUIFRC relief work consisted of food distributions. They were supplemented by some work-relief projects, such as road-building and well-digging, which were designed to provide work for famine refugees and to create lasting improvements in the physical infrastructures of affected areas. Both organizations also initiated measures to prevent epidemic outbreaks. Between 20 and 30 million Chinese were threatened with death from starvation and disease in 1920-1921. A combination of efficient intervention, rapid transmission of relief funds and supplies, and cooperation between the Chinese government and foreign relief agents held famine-related deaths to about 500,000.

When relief operations concluded in 1921, various relief committee members and workers evaluated accomplishments and offered suggestions to improve future efforts. A survey revealed that a majority of those who had been directly involved in the relief effort favored famine prevention through planned public works projects designed to generate economic improvement. Their approach appeared, in many ways, to be a convergence of Chinese traditional and emerging twentieth century foreign views. An organization known as the China International Famine Relief Commission (CIFRC) was founded in late 1921 to provide short-term emergency relief when needed and, at the same time, to implement measures for famine prevention. Commission objectives and philosophies opened a new chapter in foreign approaches to famine intervention in China.

Under more favorable circumstances, the accumulated experience and expertise might have fulfilled the dual goals of relieving and preventing famines. Furthermore, since Commis-sion membership included Chinese, it might have avoided impinging upon Chinese nationalist sentiments or becoming involved in political issues.

The CIFRC unfortunately began with severe handicaps. First, the Commission depended upon private donations for support. Since funding was unpredictable, plans for famine prevention projects could not be undertaken until adequate funds had been accumulated. Second, foreign donors who viewed relief as pure succor were reluctant to see their donations used to finance long-term projects. Third, the CIFRC adopted a policy which limited relief work to repairing damage from "natural causes" such as drought and flood. Commission members did not believe that donors would respond favorably when famine resulted in part from war-like conditions and they were concerned that, under such circumstances, relief funds would be misused by the individuals or groups responsible for the disorders. The false dichotomy between natural and man-made causes of famine thus was given credence by one of the few organizations which had the ingenuity and the authority to overcome the long-term causes of famine in China. Although CIFRC efforts were marked by a number of successes, the Commission could not surmount the problems associated with lack of funds, political strife, and massive emergency needs created by drought, flood, and war.

Despite ongoing efforts by private individuals and organizations to get help for China, outside assistance to Chinese famine victims came to a virtual halt between 1928 and 1930, when between three and seven million people died of starvation and disease. Donors were disenchanted by repeated requests for contributions, by reports on Chinese official corruption, by the confusion associated with civil war, and by the absence of a strong central government in China. When flooding caused major devastation throughout the Yangtze region in 1931, the most important foreign relief contribution to China was medical aid, which was provided through the League of Nations and which was a harbinger of relief work since undertaken by various United Nations agencies. American aid consisted of the sale of surplus grain to the Chinese government. The World War II years, discussed later in this chapter, were characterized by the American public's continued reluctance to support any but the most basic emergency relief measures for China.[1]

THE SOVIET UNION, 1920-1922

H.H. Fisher's view of conditions in parts of the Soviet Union after World War I was not unlike Richard Tawney's impression of China. Tawney wrote that the position of China's rural population was that of "a man standing up to the neck in water so that even a ripple is sufficient to drown him." Fisher wrote: "In the Volga area, where drought was a constant threat, the peasant eked out his life under a suspended sentence of death."

The years between the famines of 1891-1892 and 1921-1922 were marked by war and revolution. The land reforms carried out between 1906 and 1913 created three classes of land holdings. Some were large and some were middle sized, but others were so small that they could not support the families living on them causing the men to hire themselves out as laborers. In addition, there were a vast number of landless peasants who worked on large estates. When the war began, seventeen million men and two million draft animals were conscripted for military service and farm labor shortages resulted. Transport systems were utilized primarily for the war effort and food shipments to major cities were interrupted. Coal and iron manufacturing declined by 75% and 98% respectively between 1916 and 1921. In 1917, the Bolsheviks urged the peasants to seize land, but forbade them to keep more grain than they needed for their families. Food production suffered further declines. An estimated 80% of the population suffered from the effects of chronic hunger. Famine was a constant threat and, as in 1891, the peasantry was helpless.

In 1920, drought affected more than one million square miles of land and about 30 million people, but it was not the primary cause of the famine. The League of Nations reported in 1922 that famine resulted from earlier declines in agricultural production, the overall effects of the World War, the civil war, blockades, boycotts, and shortages of farming equipment and railway cars. Although it has been alleged that enough food had been produced in other areas to supply the famine regions, grain transfers were inhibited by political disorganization and by the government's intial refusal to admit that famine conditions existed.

Official measures, when finally undertaken, included food distributions, evacuation of famine refugees, and efforts to prevent epidemics. The measures were not successful because, in addition to inadequate transportion, relief activities were poorly coordinated and lacked support from Moscow. Outsiders learned of the famine through a series of accounts in *Pravda* which reported "mass flight" from the countryside in spring and summer 1921, told of peasants subsisting on grass, leaves, bark, and clay, and made references to cannibalism. In July, the Central Committee reported that "The Soviet Government is unable to help." One month later, Georgi Chicherin, Commissar of Foreign Affairs, announced that a famine was in progress, and a report from the British Trade Mission in Moscow estimated that 35 million people were starving. Lenin called the famine a "disaster that threatened to nullify the whole of the [Bolsheviks'] organizational and revolutionary work," and appealed for international relief. He did not expect the United States, or any other capitalist government, to offer assistance; consequently, he refused to make even a conciliatory gesture to Washington by releasing several Americans being held in Soviet prisons.

American public sentiment in 1921 was anti-communist, and official policies supported the political and economic isolation of the Soviet Union. Although it seemed unlikely, the U.S. ultimately did respond to appeals for relief. American intervention in the Soviet famine was not a direct response to Soviet government appeals, but to those of Maxim Gorky and Secretary of State Charles Evans Hughes. Gorky's appeal "To All Honest People" was made on behalf of an anti-Bolshevik famine committee in the USSR, and asked for food and medicine. Secretary of State Hughes believed that a positive American response to the crisis could, "if rightly used," lead to the liquidation of the Bolshevik regime.

Supervision of American relief operations was assigned to Secretary of Commerce Herbert Hoover. His aid to Belgium in 1914 had transformed famine relief into what Benjamin Weissman has called a resource which rivaled propaganda, diplomacy, and military force as an instrument of policy. Hoover's organizational abilities were remarkable. During his four and one-half years as head of the Committee for Relief to Belgium, he had supervised disbursements of more than 800 million dollars in relief funds and material, or more than the annual United States budget for any pre-war year since the Civil War. As Director of the American Relief Administration (ARA) he had organized the collection and distribution of approximately one billion dollars worth of food and supplies to U.S. armed forces and to the civilian populations of 22 different countries between 1917 and 1919.

Hoover perceived famine relief in terms of a large government operation which should be handled by experts and not as "welfare work" which, to him, meant the random handing out of food in bread lines. Hoover further believed that one individual should direct and coordinate relief operations, rather than international commissions or committees. According to Hoover, a basic principle of relief was that it be confined to averting actual starvation and that, once this was accomplished, it should be terminated. Despite the fact he perceived famine relief to the Soviet Union as a possible antidote to communism, Hoover refused to compromise the canons of philanthropy. Thus, American aid to the Soviet government was justified on the grounds of American humanitarianism while it was carried out in the name of anti-communism. Additional support for relief efforts derived from the fact that they offered economic benefits to American farmers staggering under grain surpluses which had caused prices to drop fifty percent in one year. Also, American industries were in a recession and businessmen saw in the Soviet Union a potential market for their surplus production.

Under Hoover's direction, the ARA used War Department funds to buy grain from American farmers. Additional funds, material, and personnel were authorized by Congress. The American Red Cross assisted with medical relief through a division of ARA, and a number of other private organizations contributed to relief efforts. Although some 10 million Russians received American aid, between three and five million people died from the combined effects of starvation and disease.

The political and economic results of American aid to the Soviet Union were as varied as the motives which had prompted it. Massive American relief efforts probably helped the Soviet government to remain in power, but they produced neither economic benefits for the United States nor gratitude from the Soviet Union. Ideological differences were only temporarily overcome, and Soviet critics later condemned the American relief mission as "an anti-Soviet intervention entirely devoid of humanitarian inspiration or effect." A more philosophical view was expressed by George Kennan:

> The best that may be said in retrospect is that, despite all the friction and difficulty, both sides got, basically, what they most wanted. The ARA did not become a source of conspiracy; the Soviet Government was not overthrown. Several million children, who would otherwise have died, were kept alive.[2]

CHINA (HONAN), 1943-1944

War was the overwhelming cause of famine in China from 1937 to 1949. American response from 1937 to 1941 was characterized by official reluctance to violate its neutrality by giving aid to China and by lack of support for private relief appeals. Some work was carried out by private organizations, but they lacked both unity and financial support. American assistance to China from 1942 to 1949 largely consisted of war materials for Chiang Kai-shek. American efforts to provide civilian aid were limited by the overriding military requirements of various allies, consequently funds were not equally distributed. Between June 1942 and June 1944, American dollars aided more than 40 million war victims in 31 countries. The U.S.S.R. received just over 18 million dollars, the United Kingdom just over 17 million, and China less than five million. American private efforts to aid Chinese civilians fell victim to conflict and confusion. The American Red Cross planned to transport and distribute medical supplies to both the military and civilians, but not to make cash or food transfers. The United China Defense (a Lend-Lease agency) furnished aid solely to the Chinese military, and the United China Relief (a group of private agencies) provided for "all other" relief and rehabilitation. The three organizations were divided on the issue of providing relief to famine victims in war zones. Only the power of the American press moved the Chinese government to initiate relief measures in Honan province.

Honan experienced both drought and flood in 1942. Military conflict kept farmers from tilling their fields and military needs reduced existing food stores. American Red Cross officials did not contemplate taking action in Honan or assisting United China Relief agents in determining what relief American agencies could provide. The first published reports on famine conditions in Honan appeared in the Chungking newspaper, *Ta Kung Pao,* in February 1943. The paper's Honan correspondent attacked the Chinese government for continuing to collect taxes in kind and for making compulsory food purchases when some 30 million people faced hunger. The Chinese government responded by suspending publication of *Ta Kung Pao* for three days and by refusing to allow foreign press correspondents to forward dispatches on famine conditions. According to reporters Theodore White and

Harrison Forman, government actions "acted like a barb on the foreign press." White and Forman proceeded to Honan to examine conditions for themselves. White filed a dispatch from Loyang where, by "pure chance" it was forwarded to New York "direct and uncensored." The *Time* magazine story infuriated Madame Chiang Kai-shek, and White was denounced in Chungking for avoiding censorship or for having collaborated with Communists to let his story "slip out."

Although the United China Relief appealed for funds, the Red Cross refused to make cash transferes for relief. The result was that no famine relief donations were transmitted from America. However within a month, the negative publicity persuaded Chiang's government to move food supplies into Honan. The Chinese military released food stores, and railway cars were diverted to make grain shipments. Despite the belated efforts, two to three million people died in Honan in 1943-1944, and another two to three million left the area. White later wondered whether massive foreign relief might have altered subsequent events. In spring 1944, the Japanese military decided to "clean out the province of Honan in preparation for their even greater push in the south." Chinese troops, who had "ravaged" Honan's civilian population while the famine raged, ran from the attack. White wrote:

> The peasants...had suffered through too many months of famine and merciless military extortion. Now they turned....It was estimated that 50,000 Chinese soldiers were disarmed by their own countrymen....With the countryside in a state of armed rebellion there was no hope at all for resistance. Within three weeks the Japanese had seized all their objectives...and a Chinese army of 300,000 men had ceased to exist.[3]

INDIA (BENGAL), 1943-1944

During the nineteenth century, official British famine policies prescribed doing enough to avoid popular uprisings and to avert mortalities which were in excess of normal. The Famine Codes provided guidelines for famine declaration and intervention, but they did not contain provisions for averting the threat of famine or for eliminating its long-term causes and effects. Furthermore, the Codes left the decision as to when famine should be declared to the discretion of local authorities who often were reluctant to take action unless conditions were extreme. The inadequacies of official policies were epitomized in the Bengal famine of 1943-1944.

Long-standing vulnerability to famine in Bengal was summarized in a Famine Commission Report issued in 1944:

> Even in normal times...considerable numbers among the poorer classes live on the margin of subsistence because they do not grow enough food and do not earn enough money to buy the amount of food they need....It is the result, not of a shortage in the total supply of food, but lack of purchasing power in the hands of the poorer classes, that is, of their poverty.

The 1943-1944 famine resulted from a variety of misfortunes. During the years 1900-1940, the grain supplies available in Bengal on a per capita basis fell from almost 600 pounds per year to about 400 pounds. By 1934, Bengal had became a net importer of food. World War II caused a steady decline in the availability of food imports. A critical point was reached in May 1942. Burma, which had been a chief source of rice imports, fell to the Japanese. At the same time, grain exports to war zones in the Middle East and Europe were increased. Fear of invasion prompted the British government to initiate a "Denial Policy" which caused the removal of all transportation equipment and rice stores from the Ganges-Brahmaputra delta. Rice cultivation in the region was halted in order to deny potential food sources to the Japanese. A "Boat Denial Policy" permitted the government to seize all boats large enough to hold ten people. Forty-six thousand craft were confiscated, thus eliminating both fishing and coastal transport. As a result, barriers were created against the movement of food, imports were either cut off or delayed, and hoarding both reduced the availability of grain supplies and caused grain prices to rise. The government was unable to coordinate internal grain procurement and distribution and, despite signs of impending famine, rice was exported from parts of Bengal in 1942.

By December 1942, food prices had doubled and, by spring 1943, they doubled or tripled again. Reports from the countryside described people going without food, increased crimes against property, desertions of wives by husbands and of children by parents, increased sales of possessions and land, and growing migrations to towns and cities. Local efforts to provide assistance were limited by the high cost of food. People who depended upon charity starved. Official efforts to control prices failed, and grain transfers into deficit zones were prevented because of hoarding by growers and because of inadequate transportaton.

The first published accounts of rural starvation appeared in the Calcutta-based English-language newspaper, *The Statesman* . The editors did not want to offend the governments of Bengal or India by publicizing a famine while the war was going on, but they felt compelled to draw attention to the fact that Calcutta was filling with beggars. *The Statesman* called for government relief measures in July 1943; but the response was negligible. The Governor of Bengal, Sir John Herbert, was dying of cancer and the Viceroy of India, Lord Linlithgow, was not concerned with Bengal. British colonies and British armed forces were to be provided with food and hence the export of grain continued.

Food became available with surprising speed when the new Viceroy, Lord Wavell, restored shipments of grain to Bengal. Almost 300,000 tons of grain reached Calcutta between October and December 1943 after railway lines were repaired. The Indian army assisted in carrying food and other relief supplies to remote villages. However, the measures were too few and too late. Deaths from starvation peaked in late summer and autumn of 1943, while overall mortality reached its highest point in December with outbreaks of dysentery, cholera, malaria, and smallpox. Deaths remained above normal for three more years because of continuing epidemic outbreaks and because the poorest citizens were unable to purchase adequate supplies of food or medicine. Official British estimates placed the number of dead at 1.5 million. Later studies suggest that between three and four million people may have died of starvation and disease.

Many critics have insisted that the Bengal famine was "man-made." Narayan called it a "man-made catastrophe aggravated by adverse visitations of nature," and Bhatia saw it as "a tragedy in unpreparedness." Ghosh referred to government responses as "shameful and cruel," while Ela Sen called the famine a political failure which resulted from official incompetence: "It was the core that was rotten and therefore the flesh had grown poisonous." Venkataramani blamed Winston Churchill for the calamity, and argued that the United States did not take concrete action on behalf of Indian famine victims because Franklin Roosevelt was reluctant to offend Churchill and because he did not believe that a gesture to the Indian people was worthwhile from either a humanitarian or from a political point of view.

America's official failure to embark upon relief efforts in India coincided with India's exclusion from United Nations Relief and Rehabilitation Administration (UNRRA) distributions because it was not a "liberated" area. Secretary of State Dean Acheson explained that UNRRA aid was restricted to war victims liberated by the allied forces in countries belonging to the United Nations. India was part of the British empire and therefore could not be included under UNRRA categories for relief.

The Bengal famine was unusual because it was not precipitated by widespread crop failures. There was no absolute shortage of grain in Bengal when the famine began. However, war conditions had a profound effect upon grain marketing and distribution, and officials ignored the signs of impending famine. The disruptions of 1942 and 1943 produced conditions usually associated with crop failures. Their effects were compounded by official failures within India and by the absence of international assistance.[4]

SUMMARY

Famine relief to China during 1921-1922 was supported by funds from the Chinese government, the Chinese people, and individual donors around the world. Although they did not offer direct government support, two American presidents encouraged private contributions. The relief efforts carried out in China were divided among two major and several minor committees. The work they did sometimes overlapped and sometimes was governed by Chinese political concerns but, in general, it was unusually successful. Furthermore, famine relief was enhanced by cooperative efforts to initiate measures for famine prevention. Relief to the Soviet Union during the same years was supported primarily by American government funds and resources. Efforts carried out in the Soviet Union were dominated by Herbert Hoover's insistence upon halting relief operations when emergency conditions seemed to be over. Despite administrative successes in providing food for several million people, the Soviet experience was characterized by political tensions on both sides, and by unfulfilled hopes for economic benefits to the United States.

American relief to China during World War II consisted largely of military aid to the government. Chinese official measures in famine intervention were carried out in response to embarrassment and outside pressure. The British government in India neither sought nor received assistance from the United States; the denial of aid through UNRRA was largely a product of American concerns with the plight of war victims in Europe.

American foreign aid assumed massive proportions during World War II, but the specific needs of famine victims were subservient to war needs and all aid was given selectively. In 1943, it became evident that major relief and rehabilitation would be needed when the war ended but, once again, aid was given selectively to Great Britain, France, Greece, and Turkey and, later, to Korea and Japan. UNRRA operations were not beneficial to India and had only moderate effects in China. Nor was the United States content to allow UNRRA to supervise post-war reconstruction independently. The American government administered relief directly in many parts of the world. In most cases it was carried out to diminish the threat of Communism.

The immediate post-war goals of international cooperation on behalf of the poor, the hungry, and the displaced were not realized. China, which had been the target of private American assistance since the nineteenth century, embarked upon an independent political course which precluded American aid. Relations with the Soviet Union became a source of tension and hostility. India won its independence from British rule, and a new Indian government had to assume control over efforts to prevent and alleviate famine conditions. Neither advances in communications and technology nor the emergence of international relief organizations succeeded in ameliorating hunger or in reducing the threat of famine.

Notes

1. For information on medical and nutritional disorders in China, and for a survey of foreign relief efforts during the first half of the 20th century, see Golkin [271]. American Red Cross relief operations are explained in the Red Cross Report [466]. PUIFRC relief work is detailed in the PUIFRC Report [476]. Results of the survey taken among relief committee members and workers is in PUIFRC [475]. Nathan [474] has written a full history of the CIFRC. Todd [480] describes several of the famine prevention projects undertaken. The problems which characterized efforts to raise funds in 1928-1930 are in the Red Cross Report [465], which explains Red Cross refusal to participate in relief efforts, and in the CIFRC report [468] which justifies CIFRC appeals for aid. Details on flood relief in 1931 are in the Republic of China Report [477].

2. Tawney [479] and Fisher [573] express similar views on marginal subsistence patterns among the rural populations of China and the Soviet Union. Fisher [573] provides a detailed historic account of ARA famine relief activities. Weissman [578] explains both American and Soviet activities; a broad summary is in Kennan [576].

3. White and Jacoby [482] provide a compelling first-hand account of the Honan famine. White [481] describes Chiang's reaction to his reports, his difficulties with *Time*, and Chinese official actions on behalf of famine victims which, according to White, were initiated by the power of the press to move officialdom. Curti [119] explains American response to appeals for relief to China and to publication of *Thunder Out of China*.

4. The Famine Commission Report was published in 1945 and reprinted in 1976 [530]. Greenough [529] provides a superb account of the 1943 famine. Sen [305, 535] supports the thesis that famine does not result only from a decline in food availability, but that famine conditions can be produced by rising food prices. Additional famine accounts are in Bhatia [513], Narayan [532], Ghosh [528], Ela Sen [536], and Venkataramani [538]. U.S. response is discussed in Wallerstein [118] and Wiseberg [333], among others; the story of UNRRA activities in other parts of the world is in Woodbridge [378].

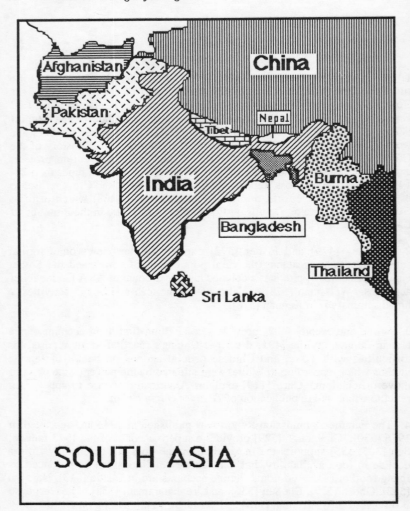

SOUTH ASIA

VI

Twentieth Century Famines, 1950 to 1980s

Famine conditions have been reported in some part of the underdeveloped world almost every year since the end of World War II. They have taken their greatest tolls in Biafra, Cambodia (Kampuchea), China, India, Mozambique, Nigeria, and Northeastern Brazil. Serious food shortages have occurred in Chad, Indonesia, the Philippines, Tanzania, and Zimbabwe. And the list is not complete. In each case, conditions have been treated as if they were new or unexpected and, despite good intentions, most relief operations have been poorly coordinated and relief organizations have been ill-equipped to meet famine needs. As William Murdoch writes:

> Public concern over world hunger ebbs and flows with the occurrence of disasters. Between these peaks of attention, however, Western nations continue to follow policies that—through ignorance and self-interest—make the situation worse.

The United Nations has been involved in most major relief efforts since the end of World War II, but has provided a relatively small percentage of the total financial assistance. Private relief organizations have raised large sums of money for any number of different relief operations. They have done so independently and, despite efforts to coordinate their activities, they have not centralized relief planning or operations. Most famine relief efforts have been funded by individual donor governments. Thus politics, or what Stephen Green calls "the dark side of relief," have played a critical role in determining targets for national and international relief aid.

An examination of the famines which occurred in Bangladesh, the Sahel, and Ethiopia during the 1970s, and in Ethiopia during the 1980s, provides vivid demonstrations of what has and has not changed in famine intervention. If it is assumed that the sole objective of famine relief is to save lives, then donors' wishes have been fulfilled. If it is understood that famine is a product of poverty, chronic hunger, and disease, and that the goals of famine relief should include measures for post-famine rehabilitation and famine prevention, then relief measures have failed. The discussion which follows provides a sad commentary on the inability of international organizations, voluntary societies, and governments to provide adequate assistance. If recent critical analyses and reports will be utilized by *all* relief organizations, and if some of their proposals can be implemented, the revitalized famine intervention programs might play a critical role in averting or relieving future episodes of famine.

BANGLADESH, 1974-1975

A low-income, low food-grain restoration began to take place among the people of Bengal after the 1943 famine. While that restoration was taking place, India was partitioned. The eastern part of Bengal became East Pakistan—renamed Bangladesh following civil war in 1970-1971. Partition produced massive in and out-migrations which continued during the 1950s and 1960s. Unemployment rose, purchasing power declined, and domestic grain production could not meet popular needs. Substantial food imports were necessary throughout the period. Severe flooding occurred in 1954, 1955, 1956, 1962, 1963, 1968, and 1969. The people were neither prepared for, nor insured against them. Famine was not declared in the wake of recurrent flooding because the government was able to provide relief in time to avert widespread starvation and because the price of food did not rise dramatically. However, vulnerability to famine conditions rose steadily.

Disagreement over the issue of regional autonomy divided East and West Pakistan during the 1960s. In mid-1970, political tensions rose over the impending elections scheduled for December. Major flooding occurred between July and September and, in November, the worst cyclone of the century occurred. Official estimates placed immediate mortality at 200,000; unofficial figures were closer to one million. A nine-month civil war began in December 1970, after East Pakistan voted overwhelmingly for regional autonomy. Food production declined dramatically, transportation was disrupted, and some 25 million people were threatened with severe food shortages. However, despite dire predictions, a major famine was avoided.

Widespread starvation was averted when the population of East Pakistan declined by almost 10 million as war refugees fled to India. The sudden population decrease, combined with income from international sales of jute, rapid conversion to rice cultivation, and intensive use of waterways to move grain, helped to avoid actual famine. In addition, the Indian government set up camps for the refugees. Ration cards were issued to families so that they could obtain food, and children were given protein supplements. An inoculation program and vigorous sanitation controls halted an outbreak of cholera. Indian government measures were supplemented by donations of medical supplies, medical equipment, tents, tarpaulins, and powdered milk from UNICEF and private relief organizations.

Bangladesh emerged from the war as an independent nation, but the return of some nine million of the war refugees placed enormous burdens on the new leaders of Bangladesh. They lacked experience in running a nation, and official funds, derived from tax collections, were insufficient to sustain even marginal subsistence among the population. The government had to divert foreign exchange credits to fill immediate food needs. Conditions worsened when rice crops failed in 1972. Transportation was inadequate to make food transfers and, even worse, the price of all imports rose sharply. A severe cyclone in December 1972 caused widespread destruction and magnified food shortages. The cost of living among factory workers rose more than 100% while real wages among agricultural workers declined by 24% to 48%.

Reports from rural areas in March 1973 told of famine food consumption, increased begging, migrations, and starvation. The government announced that the reports were exaggerated and insisted that there was no reason for alarm. However, official reassurances could not stem reports that people were consuming plantain saplings and banana leaves because they had no rice. In many regions, all edible plants were exhausted by July and diarrheal diseases were epidemic. Husbands deserted their wives and families in order to search for work. Children were sold. Prostitution and infanticide became common. Starving people, as well as dead bodies, began to fill the streets in the capital city of Dacca. In August, widespread flooding, cholera outbreaks, and reports of rising mortality made it impossible for the government any longer to deny the famine. In September 1974, the Prime Minister admitted that a famine existed and ordered food distributions. Well over four million people, or more than six percent of the population, were being fed daily from official stores by November; but government supplies were not sufficient to meet needs and international assistance was requested.

Foreign aid arrived late and at a high price. Bangladesh had been receiving regular food aid from the U.S. but, at the time of the famine, Washington had decided to halt the jute trade between Bangladesh and Cuba. After cash shortages forced Bangladesh to cancel two consecutive grain orders from an American company, Washington's demands for the trade embargo were accepted. The following incident was cited in Amartya Sen's study:

> The U.S. threatened to cut off food aid in September 1974. At that time the American ambassador called upon Dr. Nurul Islam, Chairman of Bangladesh's Planning Commission...to formally request that Bangladesh cease exporting jute to Cuba....The government of Bangladesh canceled further exports of jute to Cuba at a time when competition from Indian jute and low world market prices had substantially eroded its foreign exchange earnings.

The flow of American grain resumed after Bangladesh gave up its trade with Cuba but, by then, the worst of the famine was over. According to available figures, starvation and disease had claimed between 700,000 and 1,000,000 lives. Responsibility for the loss of life in 1974 has been since laid at several doors. First, official unwillingness to recognize famine conditions resembled the British response in 1943. Second, official actions were too late and too limited to prevent widespread starvation. Third, relief distributions were both inadequate and poorly managed. Fourth, Bangladesh sought emergency aid only for the effects of flood damage and was reluctant to publicize its famine abroad. Fifth, outside assistance was delayed by political considerations.

The international community did not respond with massive assistance until starvation had taken its enormous toll and, even then, not until the political interests of the United States had been served. In addition, relief was handicapped by simultaneous global food shortages which occurred as a result of widespread crop failures and rising fuel prices during the early 1970's. Conditions were worst in Africa.[1]

THE SAHEL, 1969-1973

Among geographers, "Sahel" describes the dry zone which borders the Sahara Desert and stretches across the widest part of Africa from the Atlantic Ocean to the Red Sea. In a political context, Sahel refers to the dry zones of six African countries—Chad, Mali, Mauritania, Niger, Senegal, and Upper Volta—which are among the poorest in the world.

The long dry spell of 1969-1973 was not an unusual climatic event for the Sahel. Nor was starvation an unusual situation for the people of the region. Drought had helped to precipitate famine conditions in 1910-1914, 1941-1942, and 1969-1973; but in 1969-1973 the effects of drought were worsened by environmental deterioration initiated by human activities. Well-digging and livestock disease control programs, carried out with foreign assistance during the 1950s and 1960s, produced a rapid increase in the animal herds that resulted in overgrazing. Medical services accelerated increases in the human population during the same period. Officials encouraged the growing of cash crops for export, rather than food grains for internal consumption, and thus reduced food supplies for both animals and humans. An external cause of food shortages in the Sahel derived from a global shortage of grain which drove world food prices up and inhibited grain imports into the Sahelian countries. The combined effects of animal and human population growth, ecological damage, declining grain production, grinding poverty, prolonged drought, and rising costs for food imports, resulted in an estimated 500,000 human deaths between 1969 and 1973 and the loss of between 40% and 60% of herds. The real death tolls may never be known because none of the Sahelian governments had undertaken a population census or kept records of births and deaths before the famine; nor did they keep accurate records while the famine was in progress.

According to available data, the people who inhabit the countries of the Sahel have a life expectancy of barely forty years. Half of their children die before reaching the age of ten. Among the cattle, half the calves die during their first year and about two-thirds of the survivors die each year thereafter. Measles was a major cause of death among children in the Sahel during ordinary times; during 1969-1973, marasmus was "common." Scurvy, beriberi, eye diseases, viral hepatitis, tuberculosis, malaria, diarrhea, bronchitis, and pneumonia were diagnosed among famine victims who made their way to refugee camps. Nutritional edema was reported among all age groups. The worst conditions were reported from Mali, Mauritania, and Niger.

Drought reports made between 1969 and 1971 did not draw a great deal of attention to the Sahel. Finally, in 1972, representatives of the United Nations World Food Programme announced that drought had become "endemic" and that it would require "special treatment." As a result of reporting delays, relief organizations did not mobilize on behalf of the Sahelian people until 1973. An "international disaster" was declared after the dry spell was six years old. Media reports in mid-summer 1973 showed pictures of emaciated nomads and dead cattle. They also showed pictures of relief foods which had been unloaded on west African docks and lines of refugees receiving grain rations which had been donated by the United States. Most of the reports did not reveal that piles of grain were being eaten by wharf rats and they did not explain that many of the refugees who received food relief in the form of sorghum distributions got violent cases of diarrhea because their systems could not digest the coarse grain.

Although relief operations began slowly, they eventually included massive shipments of food supplies as well as provisions for shelter and medical care. Their effects have been debated.

Imperato and Caldwell assigned credit to national and international efforts for averting huge death tolls. Studies by Sheets and Morris and by Wiseberg emphasized sluggishness, chaos, mismanagement, and discrimination in relief efforts. Allegations of discriminatory relief practices claimed that pastoralists in the Sahel received more help than nomads. Political regimes and famine relief camps were based in and near villages and cities, while nomadic groups were left to fend for themselves.

The Sahel eventually received more than 100 million dollars in aid from more than 20 donor countries. No effort, however, was made to eliminate the combined disorders which had accelerated the decline to famine and which had prevented relief work from being undertaken before starvation and disease became widespread. Furthermore, relief work was undertaken without contingency plans, without information on transport networks, and without reliable information concerning specific food and medical needs. The huge sums which were donated for emergency famine relief undoubtedly held down immediate famine-related mortality. By spring 1973, drought and famine in the Sahel no longer made headlines. However, the people of the Sahel still had the highest mortality rates in the world, children continued to die of measles, transportation was not improved, 40% to 60% of herds were lost to people whose livelihoods depended upon the sales of animals and animal products, and some donors were still digging boreholes to find water.

The conviction that the Sahel would continue to experience prolonged drought at regular intervals gave rise to a variety of proposals designed to avoid a repetition of the decline to famine. They included recommendations for public health programs, repair of ecological damage, afforestation, appropriate water development programs, range management, improved transport networks, and better agricultural practices. Further suggestions for protection against famine included the establishment of information systems to monitor food supplies, communicate reports on shortages, and make plans for mobilizing and coordinating food relief efforts in the event of severe shortages.

In 1974, close to 7.5 billion dollars in aid was committed to the Sahel to stimulate self-sufficiency in food through improved agricultural production. But the funds did not provide insurance against famine precipitated by drought. At the beginning of 1984, the Food and Agricultural Organization of the United Nations appealed for one million tons of food aid for the Sahel. The request was one of many which were made on behalf of millions of people in more than twenty different African nations. By the end of 1984, famine conditions in Africa once again were making headlines all over the world.[2]

ETHIOPIA, 1972-1987

Famine was recorded in Ethiopia during the ninth century; subsequently there were ten major famines between 1540 and 1742, and two more during the 1820s. Livestock disease destroyed 75% of the cattle in Ethiopia during the 1880s, and fully 90% during the 1890s, after the disease known as rinderpest was introduced inadvertently by Europeans. An estimated 30% of the population died because they could neither produce nor buy food. During the twentieth century, famines occurred in 1916-1920, 1927-1928, 1934-1935, 1957-1958, 1964-1965, and in 1972-1973. The conditions which were displayed on the front pages of newspapers and on television screens around the world in 1984-1986 were neither new nor unusual.

During the 1950s and 1960s, increased investments were made in roads, agriculture, education and health. Despite famine conditions in some parts of the country, farming was developed in regions near the new roads and new agricultural technology was introduced by Swedish, American and World Bank projects. Large plantations which produced cash crops were established and private investors supported the production of coffee, oil seed, and grain crops. Trade expanded; however, the changes brought problems along with benefits. Common lands were fenced off and tenants were evicted. Localized famines occurred in 1957-1958 and in 1964-1965, when nearly half the population of Wollo Province died of hunger. Ecological destruction negated advances in agricultural production. Between 1965 and 1985, Ethiopia's forest cover was reduced from sixteen percent to four percent of the total area. The result was excessive erosion that turned fertile areas into semi-deserts. As the land became less productive, farmers had to sell their tools in order to buy water from neighbors who had wells. The poorest farmers, left with neither tools nor water, starved. The people who were affected most were those who farmed in areas which formerly had been used by pastoralists and which had only been under cultivation since the turn of the century.

A comprehensive nutritional survey done during the late 1950s revealed a high incidence of kwashiorkor, endemic goiter, and parasitic diseases. The effects of undernutrition were exacerbated by vitamin A deficiencies and a high incidence of gastroenteritis. Rickets was diagnosed among 30% of school children, many of whom also had sub-normal levels of vitamin A and vitamin C. Few among the population of Ethiopia had the food, the money or the nutritional reserves needed to survive the effects of acute food deficit.

First Phase, 1972-1973
The rains failed in the eastern part of Wollo Province and crops dried up in 1972. Migrations began in January 1973. The poorest people moved first. Then small landowners pawned, sold, or simply deserted their holdings. Many of them made their way to understaffed, poorly supplied relief camps. By summer, an estimated 500,000 people had died of starvation. Emperor Haile Selassie suppressed early reports of famine conditions, refused to appeal for international aid, and even continued to export agricultural products. Government aid did not begin to reach the stricken region until autumn 1973. When international aid was requested in spring 1974, it was delayed by the need to locate and organize food shipments and distributions. By the time shipments were underway, crops were being harvested again.

The famine of 1972-1973 was followed by revolution and by attempts at land reform but, according to agricultural experts, the Mengistu government, which took power after Selassie's overthrow, did little to improve access to food supplies. Neither government succeeded in controlling overgrazing or in reducing the practice of burning wood to make charcoal. Nor was anything substantive done to reduce vulnerability to starvation when crops failed or to avert the decline to famine when food was either too scarce or too expensive to sustain life.[3]

Second Phase, 1980-1987

Rainfall dwindled and severe hunger began to spread in Ethiopia in 1980. Famine was predicted early in 1982, but the Ethiopian government did not acknowledge the possibility. By the end of 1984, televised reports began to draw world attention to famine conditions in Ethiopia and, in February 1985, relief agencies reported that an estimated seven million people were affected by famine , that 2.5 million were in immediate danger of death, and that more than two million were homeless.

Many Western relief specialists, as well as reporters, were critical of the Mengistu regime. They argued that drought conditions in Ethiopia would not have precipitated widespread famine if the government had not spent hard currency for weapons to fight rebel movements. They noted that, while Ethiopia was one of the poorest countries in the world, it had the largest army in sub-Saharan Africa. In addition, Ethiopian policies dictated that government marketing boards would purchase food from farmers at low fixed prices, sell it at higher prices, and use the difference, along with foreign aid, to support military purchases, construction of office buildings and conference centers, and salaries for civil servants and workers in government-owned factories. In many ways, government policies were responsible for a twenty year decline in food production which had more negative effects than the much-publicized drought conditions. When the drought began, there were no funds for internal relief or for international food purchases, and no choice but to turn to the international community for help. Further criticisms were directed at government treatment of the populations of Eritrea and Tigray, where civil war had broken out in 1962 and 1967, respectively, as a result of Haile Selassie's annexations. Neither province had experienced any development. Officials in both regions claimed that Ethiopian military offensives had destroyed crops and that the Ethiopian government had withheld relief supplies donated by foreign voluntary organizations. An Oxfam report written in January 1984 stated:

> ...the irony of this guerrilla struggle, in which both sides are putting their political and military objectives first, is that the long war which has put a stop to reafforestation [sic] and other soil conservation

techniques may mean that the prize for victory is an infertile wasteland.

The Ethiopian people responded to the famine by reducing food consumption and then by eating wild plants, some of which caused severe vomiting, diarrhea, swelling, and jaundice. A traditional famine food known as "false banana" (a tree which did not bear fruit) was denied them because the government previously had ordered the trees removed to make room for other plants. During earlier periods of crop failure, the roots of the tree had provided emergency sustenance. Without it, thousands starved. Responses to acute food deficit differed among Ethiopian tribes. Some of them automatically provided first for their young, while others favored able-bodied adults and those who were best equipped to resume work for the community in the wake of famine. Most early migrants were men in search of work. The women stayed behind and cared for their children in accordance with the traditional practice of keeping sick children in their homes to avoid the "evil eye." However, persistent hunger eventually drove them to refugee camps.

Outsiders neither questioned nor considered the differences among indigenous practices. The tradition of feeding women and children first was re-stated by a relief worker in Ethiopia: "Who gets food first is non-negotiable." However, the care of women and children presented difficulties for relief workers. Once they were admitted to relief camps with waterproof tents, street lights, generators, and free food supplies, they devised ways to remain in them. Women with children engaged in "nutritional sabotage" in order to stay in the camps. Some mothers deliberately kept one child in a state of extreme hunger so that the entire family would not be discharged. Others engaged in "child markets" which "rented" starving children to adults who were desperate for admission into the camps. A relief worker who explained the "coping mechanisms" suggested that they were designed to ensure survival and that foreign agents might do well to strengthen the mechanisms rather than impose outside values.

New York Times reporter Clifford May concluded that Ethiopian prospects for improved food production, or for any reduction in the prospects for future famines, were slim. The record for development projects in Africa was not promising. Factories had broken down or closed, roads and railways had not been maintained, and dams had filled with silt. Well-digging had lowered water tables and, at the same time, had allowed livestock herds to grow so large that they stripped vegetation and turned grazing areas into deserts. Trees that were part of reforestation projects were chopped down at night by people who had no other fuel sources. Public works projects took desperate farmers away from their land during planting seasons. Imported foods drove down the prices of local products, and farmers had no reason to grow a surplus. Those who did grow surplus grain and attempt to store it were prosecuted by the government for hoarding.

Representatives of relief organizations had to work with government officials who had contributed to the creation of famine conditions while recognizing that, if they denied aid on the basis of government failures, they would be punishing the victims of famine and not its perpetrators. Wars in Ethiopia, Sudan, Chad, Mozambique, and Angola may have done more to precipitate famine than drought, but their effects upon agricultural production and upon the men and women who produce food cannot be catalogued with any degree of accuracy. It is generally accepted that, in 1984-1985, African farmers produced less food than they had during 1964-1965. Sixty percent of all Africans lived below poverty lines established by the World Bank, and projections indicated that the figure would rise to 80% by 1995.

Drought affected 21 countries and an estimated 150 million people in Africa between 1980 and 1985. On January 3, 1985 President Reagan announced a one billion dollar emergency program for Africa which was to be divided into food aid, non-food aid, refugee aid, and new activities. Additional donations were made by CARE, Catholic Relief Services, Africare, World Vision, and the Red Cross, along with several governments and dozens of multilateral institutions. A United Nations Office of Emergency Operations in Africa was established to coordinate donor activities, arrange the timing and amount of distributions, and help with the logistics of collecting, transporting, and administering relief supplies.

Between one and two million Ethiopian people died of starvation and disease between 1984 and 1986. United Nations representatives have predicted that the final death toll in East Africa may reach between two and five million. The full measure of international relief to Ethiopia and other African nations affected by drought and famine has not been quantified as of this writing. The headlines have ceased to convey a sense of emergency. The American public no longer reguarly sees babies dying on their television screens. However, there is no evidence that conditions in Ethiopia, or in some 20 other African countries, have returned to their pre-famine state and, even when they do, there is no reason to assume that famine will not occur again. If anything, it should be expected within the next decade.[4]

SUMMARY

The famines which have been described in this chapter occurred in parts of the world where they had long histories, where civil wars had detrimental effects upon agricultural production and economic growth, and where government failures to proclaim famines delayed relief efforts. In each case, international response fell short of filling needs for political reasons or because of global food shortages, and high food and fuel prices. Most relief efforts were directed toward halting starvation. Suggestions for long-term famine prevention were set forth but not acted on because of a lack of funding and a lack of national and international political will to carry them out. Individual donors and donor organizations were, for the most part, content with saving lives and did not insist that their relief funds be invested in projects designed to eliminate the root causes of famine. The limited number of development projects undertaken before widespread starvation began were either too narrow in scope to help avert the decline to famine, or they had negative long-term effects.

Famines cannot be understood in terms of accidents of nature or as independent events that temporarily disrupt food production, distribution, and consumption. All forms of food deficit, whether chronic or acute, have complex origins. Their elimination requires long-term planning which must be accompanied a combination of medical, nutritional, technological, economic, and political innovations.

Notes

1. Several studies on famine in Bangladesh are listed in bibliographic entries 545-551. Additional sources include Ch. 7 in Alamgir [296], Sen [303, 304, 305], and Aykroyd [286]. Case studies are included in Chen [545], Boyce & Hartmann [93], Seaman & Holt [303] and Clay [547]. American response is explained in Stanley [114], Toma [115], Vengroff & Yung [117], and Wallerstein [118].

2. Sources on famine in the Sahel are listed in bibliographic entries 419-431. In addition, see Ball [89], Dow [320], Garcia and Garcia & Escudero [300, 301], Wiseberg [333], and U.S. Government Reports [13-17].

3. Liam Nolan [400] called famine in Ethiopia during the early 1970's "the forgotten famine" because it drew limited national and international attention. Bibliographic entries 395-402 survey available literature and provide a sense of the continuing of misery which culminated in the famine of the mid 1980s.

4. The full story of famine in Ethiopia, or of famine over much of Africa, during the mid-1980s has yet to be written. Bibliographic entries 403-411 review conditions in Ethiopia. In addition, see May [344, 345, 369, 435] for examples of the excellent coverage which was published in the *New York Times*. Hardy [144] and Lancaster [95] survey Africa's economic problems; Heisel [144] writes on the relationship between population and food problems. A great deal of excellent material appeared in newspapers, weekly news magazines and journals throughout the period from late 1984-1986.

VII

Hunger and the Decline to Famine

The following discussion of hunger-related disorders is designed to provide a background for understanding the terminology which has been used to describe both hungry and starving populations. It explains how chronic food deficiency disorders, endemic diseases, and concurrent susceptibility to infectious diseases, create a vulnerability to starvation and thereby accelerate the decline to famine. When intervention consists only of emergency measures designed to halt starvation, and when chronic disorders are allowed to persist, the stage is set for recurrent episodes of famine.

Precise figures for the incidence of specific hunger-related disorders do not exist. However, most experts agree that some form of chronic hunger affects as many as one billion people in the world today, that it is mankind's most prevalent disorder, and that it causes millions to live in what Garcia and his colleagues call a state of "constant catastrophe." In most cases, poverty is the root cause of hunger. The most important means of eliminating hunger-related disorders is to improve general economic status, to expand the quantity and the quality of diets, and to provide nutritional education and medical care.

The terms malnutrition, undernutrition, and starvation appear interchangeably and without explanation in descriptions both of chronic hunger and of famine. However, they are not the same. Malnutrition and undernutrition are specific kinds of food deficiency disorders. Starvation is an extreme form of hunger which gives rise to other acute and often fatal disorders. Infectious diseases worsen the effects of each. It is probable that deaths from the combined effects of chronic hunger and infectious diseases have outnumbered deaths from starvation during most periods of famine.

MALNUTRITION

Malnutrition results from different vitamin and mineral (micronutrient) deficiencies, which produce specific clinical disorders. Their severity depends upon both the degree and the duration of deprivation. Most deficiency disorders are multiple; pure malnutrition in the form of a single deficiency disease seldom occurs outside of laboratories. In some instances, the disorders produced by malnutrition have ecological origins. In others, they may be enhanced by cultural preferences and prejudices. In most cases, they are produced by poverty which is primarily responsible for inadequate or poorly balanced diets.

Beriberi

Beriberi is caused by thiamin (vitamin B_1) deficiency. The clinical manifestations of beriberi fall into three categories: neurologic, cardiovascular, and cerebral. The neurologic form ("dry beriberi") affects peripheral nerves and produces muscle cramps and loss of sensation in the lower extremities. "Wet beriberi," the cardiovascular form, causes reduced cardiac output, pulmonary congestion, and shortness of breath. Heart failure and death may result. The cerebral form of beriberi can produce encephalitis and degeneration of cerebral nerve structures. Affected individuals become confused and unable to communicate. Their eye muscles become paralyzed; coma may be followed by death.

The highest incidence of beriberi always occurs among people for whom rice is the major source of calories and for whom thiamin rich foods such as pork, legumes and whole grains are not available. Although rice is an excellent source of calories and has a relatively high protein content, it cannot be considered a complete food. Rice lacks vitamins A and C, and its thiamin content is extremely low. The limited thiamin content of rice is further reduced by milling, storage, and preparation for cooking.

Machine-milled rice goes through a process which removes both outer and inner husk, leaving only the white grain. Since most thiamin is present in the husk, it is lost to the consumer in the milling. Furthermore, humidity, lack of fresh air and insects can reduce the thiamin content of rice by half. Prolonged soaking and vigorous washing before cooking also can result in the loss of thiamin when it is either dissolved or removed mechanically.

Thiamin requirements increase in direct proportion to the lack of fat in the diet. Thus, thiamin needs are increased when rice furnishes the majority of calories in the diet and the consumption of fatty foods is limited. Beriberi was a major cause of death in the rice-eating provinces of China before 1949, especially when vegetable crops failed and people were too poor to supplement their diets with thiamin-rich foods.

Pellagra

Niacin deficiency produces pellagra. The disorder is characterized by a sore and red tongue, disturbances of the alimentary tract, dermatitis, and changes in the nervous system. Pellagra has occurred worldwide among people whose diets contain an excessive proportion of corn. Niacin is present in corn, but in a form which is not readily absorbed by the body. The disease occurs when a diet consisting predominantly of corn is not supplemented by niacin-rich foods such as meat, fish, and wheat. Pellagra has had its highest incidence in Italy, Spain, the southern United States, China, and India. The disorder still occurs in Egypt and in other parts of Africa.

Scurvy

The deficiency disorder known as scurvy results from an inadequate intake of vitamin C (ascorbic acid), which is found in citrus fruits, green peppers, potatoes, turnips, radishes, onions, and cabbage. Victims become restless and experience a loss of appetite. They have sore mouths, bleeding gums, loose teeth, black and blue marks on their skin, and swollen joints. Scurvy can occur among individuals whose diets appear adequate, because vitamin C is destroyed by improper food handling. Prolonged cooking of foods which are rich in vitamin C negates their antiscorbutic properties. When vegetables or fruits are cut and left exposed to air, oxidation occurs and their vitamin C content is diminished.

Before the need for citrus foods in the diet was discovered, scurvy was a major problem among men who spent months at sea. It was also found to be common in the northern cities of Europe and parts of Asia where fresh produce was in limited supply. Scurvy has been recorded among famine refugees whose relief diets consisted largely of grain.

Vitamin A Deficiency

Vitamin A deficiency results from a prolonged deprivation of foods rich in vitamin A, such as animal livers, milk products which contain fat, and fish liver oils. The best plant sources for vitamin A are yellow-colored fruits and vegetables in which vitamin A exists as carotenoids (provitamin A), which are converted to vitamin A by the small intestine and stored in the liver. When the aforementioned foods are insufficient or absent from the diet, signs of deficiency appear .

The first sign, commonly called known as "night blindness," is the functional impairment of the retina. In more advanced stages, vitamin A deficiency produces dryness of the cornea which is called keratomalacia. The term xerophthalmia designates the entire deficiency syndrome in which eye lesions predominate. Persons with xerophthalmia have dry, opaque corneas, with small erosions or perforations. Permanent eye damage and even blindness can result if they are not treated. The presence of hookworm or other intestinal parasites inhibits absorption of vitamin A, while severe infections can precipitate acute vitamin A deficiency even when the diet seems to be adequate. Vitamin A deficiency remains a problem in India, Indonesia, Bangladesh, Vietnam, the Philippines, Central America, northeastern Brazil, and parts of Africa.

Vitamin A induced blindness can be prevented by the oral administration of 100,000 units of vitamin preparation twice a year, at a cost of a few cents per person. However, this is not being done. According to Thylefors, there are 28 million blind people in the world. Among the two-thirds of them who live in underdeveloped countries, fully 75% of blindness is preventable or curable.

Vitamin D Deficiency

Vitamin D is crucial to the metabolism of calcium and phosphorus in the body. The interactions among the three micronutrients are such that the metabolic effects of calcium and phosphorus deficiencies are less evident when vitamin D requirements are met. When they are not, skeletal disorders can result. The metabolic bone diseases resulting from vitamin D deficiency are called rickets in children and osteomalacia in adults. Both disorders result from the same set of dietary deficiencies, but differ in their actual manifestations because of differences between growing bones and formed bones. Infants with rickets are restless and sleep poorly. They do not sit, crawl, or walk early. When they do begin to stand, weight-bearing causes their bones to bend and produces bowlegs and deformities of the chest, spine, and pelvis. Among adults, osteomalacia causes the bones to soften and results in bowing of the long bones, shortening of the vertebrae, and flattening of the pelvic bones.

Vitamin D can be obtained from foods such as butter, egg yolks, liver, and fatty fish. It can also be obtained from exposure to sunshine. Deficiency disorders are most severe among individuals whose diets lack vitamin D and who, at the same time, have insufficient exposure to sunshine and inadequate intake of calcium-rich foods such as milk, cheese, dark green vegetables, and dried legumes. Rickets has been common among urban children who have no exposure to sunshine and whose diets an otherwise inadequate. A significant incidence of osteomalacia occurs among adult Muslim women who wear veils which protect them from sunshine and who do not have adequate diets. The disorders do not exist where milk is fortified by vitamin D.

Endemic Goiter

Lack of iodine in the diet produces the thyroid gland disorder known as endemic or simple goiter. The disease, which occurs primarily in areas where soil and water have a low iodine content, produces the physical and mental forms of retardation known as cretinism. Iodine is present in most food materials and in water, but amounts vary from region to region. There is more iodine in plant than animal foods, and more in fruits than grains. Marine plants contain more iodine than fresh-water varieties, and marine algae are especially rich in iodine. Marine fish and shellfish, dairy products and many vegetables are good sources of iodine.

Endemic goiter can be prevented entirely with the use of iodized salt. Although prevention is both simple and inexpensive, the disease affects as many as 200 million people in today's world. It has its greatest incidence in the inland regions of Central Africa, in Northeastern Brazil and other mountainous regions of South America, and in the Himalayan regions.

Nutritional Anemia

Nutritional anemia occurs as a result of either iron or folic acid deficiency. Although its causes are usually multiple, most cases are produced by an inadequate intake of iron-rich foods or they occur in association with severe parasitic disorders such as malaria, hookworm, and other kinds of infestations.

Summary

Although great progress has been made toward eliminating beriberi, pellagra, and scurvy, each of them has played a critical role in magnifying death rates during periods of extreme hunger. Diseases associated with the lack of vitamins A and D, iodine, and iron still have a very high incidence in many parts of the world. Popular emphasis upon caloric needs can obscure the fact that malnourished people may be consuming enough calories to maintain body weight, while suffering from the effects of inadequate micronutrient intake. Caloric deficits, or the inadequate intake of proteins, fats, and carbohydrates, produce the form of hunger known as primary undernutrition.[1]

UNDERNUTRITION

Undernutrition occurs in two forms: primary undernutrition and secondary undernutrition. Primary undernutrition results from insufficient calories which are provided by proteins, fats, and carbohydrates—known as macronutrients. Secondary undernutrition is produced by gastrointestinal infections and infestations. Both forms of undernutrition lead to physical debilitation, susceptibility to infectious diseases, and reduced life expectancy.

Primary Undernutrition

Proteins, fats, and carbohydrates (macronutrients) produce energy and take part in the structural makeup of the body. Macronutrients are degraded into simpler compounds by digestion. Within the body, they create essential amino acids, fatty acids, and glucose. Carbohydrates and fats spare tissue protein. When they are not available in sufficient amounts, efficient protein utilization cannot occur and considerably more protein is required to maintain a positive protein balance. A general lack of macronutrients is manifested in loss of body weight, diminished physical energy, and increased susceptibility to infectious diseases.

Caloric requirements are usually determined by age, sex, occupation, body size and composition, climate, and other ecological factors. Severe deficiencies can produce disorders which are usually described as protein-calorie malnutrition (PCM), and which are often associated with starvation. Among children, the most severe forms of PCM are marasmus and kwashiorkor. Although both conditions are identified regularly among victims of chronic undernutrition, they are seldom given publicity until their victims are also victims of famine.

Secondary Undernutrition

Secondary undernutrition results from gastrointestinal infections and infestations which have adverse effects upon caloric intake and protein metabolism. They produce a variety of debilitating disorders, reduce life expectancy, and often are a direct cause of death. Inadequate sanitation, improper disposal of human excreta, and failure to wear shoes both produce and exacerbate the problems in areas where secondary undernutrition takes its greatest tolls. When entire communities are affected, generalized weakness and inability to work reduces overall productivity. Different kinds of infestations produce different symptoms. They include bloody diarrhea, abdominal cramping, bowel obstruction, loss of protein, anemia, heart disease, and blindness.

Secondary undernutrition has an enormous worldwide incidence. Some 350 million people live where malaria is rampant, and another 850 million reside where it has only been partly controlled. Malaria alone causes an estimated two million deaths each year. Some 300 million people living in Southeast Asia have elephantiasis. As many as one in twenty people in Africa, and more than 300 million people worldwide, have schistosomiasis. Approximately one billion people worldwide, have hookworm. Their conditions are such that not even adequate caloric intake can compensate for the debilitating effects of the infestations. The combined effects of chronic disease and chronic debilitation result in the inability to grow or to purchase needed food, as well as in a predisposition to other forms of disease.

The importance of secondary undernutrition as a cause of debilitation and death cannot be overemphasized. Each of the aforementioned disorders, which provide only a few examples of the problem, has its highest incidence among people whose diets are marginal, whose living conditions do not afford basic sanitary measures, whose incomes do not permit drugs to treat their disorders, and whose governments cannot or will not invest in measures for disseminating existing remedies, discovering new ones, or developing preventive measures.

Ironically, several efforts to control secondary undernutrition have been undermined by technologiy designed to aid its victims. Pesticides have produced resistant organisms. Development projects, such as irrigation works, have expanded their habitat. Insecticides have poisoned food supplies, and anti-malarial agents have become ineffective as malarial parasites have become resistant to therapeutic remedies.

Chronic Hunger and Infectious Diseases

People who suffer from chronic hunger have poor resistance to infectious diseases and infectious diseases exaggerate the effects of chronic hunger. Their interactions can produce serious complications or fatal consequences. Vitamin C deficiency can be precipitated by parasitic disorders, tuberculosis, typhoid fever, and viral infections. Beriberi can follow infections among individuals with marginal thiamin levels. Signs of vitamin A deficiency are worsened by any infectious process. Medical experts have stated that most deaths among the poorest people of the world can be attributed to the combined effects of hunger and infectious diseases.

Hunger & Fertility

The relationships among chronic hunger, poverty and population growth are controversial ones. Questions have been raised regarding the effects of chronic hunger-related disorders or fecundity (reproductive capacity), and fertility (actual reproduction). Studies by Bongaarts and by Menken and his colleagues reveal that moderate chronic malnutrition has only a minor effect upon fecundity and that the resulting decrease in fertility is very small. Thus there is little evidence that chronic hunger reduces birth rates. At the same time, one of the reasons that birth rates among the poor and hungry are so high is that many of the new-born do not survive. When they do, they are considered economic assets by people whose life expectancy is limited and for whom economic productivity is limited by chronic hunger and disease.[2]

Malnutrition & Undernutrition: a Summary

It is possible that as many as half the children in the underdeveloped world are inadequately nourished. An estimated 200,000 children are blinded each year because of vitamin A deficiency alone. One in ten infants in the underdeveloped world dies before reaching the age of one, compared with one in fifty in the developed world. Worldwide figures indicate that some 40,000 children die every day from the combined effects of chronic hunger and infectious diseases and that another 40,000 are disabled because of them.

Life expectancy among adults in underdeveloped countries ranges from 45 to 51 years, compared with 72 years in developed nations. More than one billion people, or roughly one-fourth of the world's population, have a per capita income of less than 300 dollars per year, and control barely three percent of the world's wealth. They suffer the most from diseases associated with inadequate micronutrient intake, from primary and secondary undernutrition, and from infectious diseases.

Despite their widespread incidence, the disorders associated with chronic hunger have not given rise to massive emergency relief efforts because hunger-related disorders lack drama and because they are seldom listed as direct causes of death. However, they do contribute in large measure to early mortality during normal times, and greatly magnify death rates during periods of acute food deficit. Since poorly nourished people have limited physical and economic reserves, they are the first to sicken and die when famine occurs. If they survive, their prospects for full recovery are severely limited by the effects of physical and economic disabilities which both precede and accompany famine conditions.

STARVATION

Man has developed adaptive mechanisms in the form of energy reserves to help him survive periods of extreme hunger. Among individuals who have been well fed, physiologic reserves can avert death from starvation for two months or longer as their bodies adjust to steady weight losses. Consumption of small amounts of proteins and carbohydrates will permit them to function normally until about 10% of their body weight has been lost. Their bodies then begin to make downward adjustments in energy demands. As body weight is reduced, fewer calories are required to sustain physical activity. At the same time, a curtailment of normal activity occurs which explains why the rate of weight loss declines during periods of semistarvation, and why life can be sustained for prolonged periods of time on relatively small amounts of food. People who have limited nutritional reserves can exhaust them within two days when food is absent. They are the first to starve.

Actual starvation, the most severe form of hunger, is manifested in extreme physical depletion. It is the paramount sign of famine when it occurs on a wide scale. Individuals who are starving complain of weakness, hunger pains, dizziness, blackouts, and increased urinary frequency. They are depressed, irritable, withdrawn, and emotionally unstable. They become emaciated. Their skin develops the consistency of paper, becomes dull and inelastic, and may show dusty brown splotches. Their hair becomes dry, lackluster, and sparse. Women experience amenorrhea and men become impotent. Pregnancy rates decline and miscarriages increase. People who are starving have slow pulse rates and low blood pressures. Emaciation may be masked by the insidious onset of edema, or swelling of the body. The intestinal wall becomes thin and loses its ability to absorb nutrients. Death from starvation usually occurs when about one-third of the body weight has been lost. Intractable diarrhea is the most common terminal event. The earliest deaths from starvation usually occur among the very young and the elderly.

People who are not familiar with the physical manifestations of starvation have been surprised at the absence of acute vitamin deficiency disorders among the starving. The absence of such disorders has been attributed, by implication, to the availability of vitamins released by the body as a result of the breakdown of body tissues. Another reason may be related to the general slowing down of body processes during the course of starvation, which reduces the vitamin requirements. It is generally agreed that, when vitamin deficiencies do occur among starving people, they result more from marked alterations in diet than from a general caloric deficit. This has been particularly true in the case of scurvy. A serious outbreak occurred during the Irish famine of the 1840s, when relief food consisted largely of corn meal which lacked the vitamin C normally provided by potatoes. Another episode was recorded in China in 1935, when relief food consisted primarily of mixed cereals and vegetables were absent. Sahelian famine refugees in the 1970s suffered from both scurvy and beriberi, and there were reports of vitamin A deficiency among Ethiopians in the mid-1980s. Paradoxically, vitamin intake may increase in communities accustomed to a limited diet when, during periods of acute food deficit, the diet is expanded to include wild berries, fruits, and green leafy plants.

In addressing the need for vitamins as part of famine relief, de Ville de Goyet wrote: "The distribution of multivitamin tablets to the entire population of the affected area is a waste of time and money. The best means of providing vitamins is an adequate diet." While his assessment is essentially correct, famine relief workers have found that vitamin and mineral supplements, as well as extra protein rations, have accelerated recovery when they were added to relief diets.

Starvation-Related Disorders

Certain disorders have been associated with starvation for centuries, but have been understood only in recent years. They include nutritional edema, kwashiorkor, and marasmus.

(Nutritional Edema)

Famine accounts throughout history mention the edema, or swelling, that occurred among people who were starving. Most noted the striking association between the presence of edema and subsequent death from starvation. Medical observers described how the swelling began in dependent parts and spread slowly to the rest of the body. They further noted that edema often masked emaciation by giving victims' faces a bloated appearance. More recent investigations have revealed that nutritional edema is caused by an extreme shortage of calories, pre-existing cardiac or renal disease, severe protein deficiency, dysentery, and anemia resulting from parasitic infestations. Keys and colleagues noted that the most extensive incidence of edema during famine periods has occurred where disorders such as malaria and dysentery were combined with a starvation diet superimposed upon a pre-existing poor nutritional state.

(Marasmus)

Marasmus, a term derived from the Greek expression "to waste away," is usually used to describe extremely emaciated infants with stick-like limbs, wide eyes, and the loose, wrinkled skin usually associated with old age. The disorder results from severe macronutrient deficiency and is often accompanied by anemia, diarrhea, and dehydration.

(Kwashiorkor)

Kwashiorkor usually occurs among children who are between eighteen months and three years of age. The disorder is believed to result from a lack of specific amino acids, with overall protein and caloric deficiencies as common contributing factors. Among young children, prominent symptoms include retarded growth, apathy, loss of appetite, and diarrhea. Adult victims are weak and apathetic. They have wasted muscles and poor appetites. Kwashiorkor can be both precipitated and complicated by bacterial and viral infections. The most dramatic signs of kwashiorkor are bloating, which appears incongruous with starvation, and changes in victims' hair color and texture, which is most pronounced among dark-haired people. The characteristic changes in hair color take place in a progression from black to orange to yellow, while hair texture becomes thin and dry as well as straight. Kwashiorkor is so linked with depigmentation of the hair that its incidence among famine victims often can be determined by description rather than by diagnosis.

Kwashiorkor has had its greatest incidence in tropical Africa, where the dietary mainstays consist of high carbohydrate foods such as yams, cassava, and plantain. Extensive outbreaks have been recorded during periods of civil war and social disruption. In many instances, children suffering from nutritional edema have signs of both kwashiorkor and marasmus. When hospitalized, some 20% of affected children die of infections, anemia, hypoglycemia, hypothermia, cardiac failure, or liver damage.

Starvation & Epidemic Diseases
Starvation and epidemic diseases occur together for two reasons. First, extreme hunger impairs defense mechanisms and increases susceptibility to disease. Second, the social disruption, crowding, lack of sanitation, and virtual absence of medical facilities, which are characteristic among starving communities, accelerate the spread of diseases. The combination results in epidemic outbreaks.

Typhus, or "famine fever," was a major cause of famine deaths in Europe. Smallpox and cholera have taken uncounted lives during periods of famine in Asia. Plague, diphtheria, typhoid, whooping cough, scarlet fever, measles, and tuberculosis also have been associated with famine deaths for centuries. During recent decades, African famine victims have died of bronchitis, cholera, diarrhea, measles, and pneumonia as well as from the effects of extreme undernutrition. Historical records of famine conditions have not distinguished deaths caused by starvation from deaths due to epidemic disease. However, a United Nations Food and Agricultural Organization (FAO) report published in 1967 expressed a growing consensus that, during most periods of famine, deaths from epidemic diseases have exceeded deaths from starvation.

Although the association between famine and epidemic diseases has a lengthy history, there have been exceptions. Despite widespread starvation, no major epidemics developed in Greece in 1942 or in Holland in 1945 where early attention to sanitation and disease prevention reduced the risk of epidemic outbreaks, and where prompt medical response to signs of impending epidemics reduced both the impact and the death rate of the famine.

SUMMARY

The causes and persistence of chronic hunger and endemic and infectious diseases make the links between malnutrition, undernutrition, and famine dangerous throughout vast areas of Africa, India, Latin America, the Middle East, and Southeast Asia. So-called "normal hunger" may account for as many as thirteen to eighteen million deaths each year. The threat of famine is widespread and ominous because of conditions that much of the world accepts as an ordinary state. The problem has been summarized by Frederik Bang:

> Famine usually occurs as a sudden acute shortage of food in an area where malnutrition due to poverty and nutritional ignorance already exists, and where there is already a narrow margin between available food and nutritional demand.

Although there are major differences between chronic hunger and famine, failure to recognize and to eliminate the links between them, or to alleviate the poverty that has permitted them to occur, has inhibited understanding famine and developing coherent programs for famine relief and prevention. [4]

Notes

1. A number of sources which explain medical disorders associated with malnutrition are listed in the bibliography. Others are readily available. Malnutrition can be identified by means of dietary surveys, clinical examinations, anthropomorphic (body) measurements, or biochemical testing. Evaluations are most accurate when the above means are used in combination. The absence of facilities for identifying malnutrition in underdeveloped countries makes it difficult to achieve accuracy in measuring the true extent of malnutrition. Thus, figures are estimates based upon available clinical data.

Another means for judging the extent of hunger and disease related disorders is to measure the Infant Mortality Rate for a given region or nation. The Infant Mortality Rate (IMR) is determined by measuring the number of infants per 1,000 who die before reaching one year of age. An IMR above 50 is evidence that chronic hunger and endemic diseases are a widespread problem. For example, the IMR in both Sweden and Japan is 7. In the United States, it is 11. The figure for India is 122, which represents a decline from 157 in 1960. Upper Volta has an IMR of 210. When IMR figures fall below 50, they provide good evidence for improved popular welfare and signal an end to hunger as a persistent, pervasive, chronic problem. China, for instance, had an IMR of 125 in 1950. In 1985 it dropped to 44 as a result of improved nutrition and health care services.

2.   Sources for information on primary undernutrition are numerous. Passmore [223] and Passmore & Davidson [224] explain disorders in lay terms. Secondary undernutrition is a vast and complex problem. The term encompasses multiple disorders which are not fully understood and which cannot be fully controlled with existing medicines. Bibliographic entries 240-251 provide introductory materials; their contents emphasize the need for intensive research into preventions and cures.

3.   The specific relationships between hunger and infectious diseases and between starvation and epidemics, remain a topic for serious investigation. Several points of view are represented in bibliographic entries 252-262 and 280-285. The "classic" work on starvation is by Keys et al. [273], whose compilation of historic materials on the medical, social and psychological problems associated with starvation, and whose clinical experiments with human subjects, is unique to the field. Additional sources are listed in bibliographic entries 267-279. In many cases, the contents of the materials noted above overlap.

4.   The conviction that hunger is the greatest problem in the world today is set forth by several authors in studies which include Garcia and Garcia & Escudero [300, 301], Greenwood & Edwards [172], Masefield [292], and Pearson & Greenwell [225]. The statement by Bang [335] represents a consensus.

VIII

Selected Bibliography

This bibliography is designed to provide an introduction to the broad problems associated with hunger and famine, and to facilitate access to famine studies. The contents are not definitive, but have been chosen for the diverse views and coverage they represent.

The materials have been divided into five major categories: I. World Food Problems, II. World Hunger, III. Famine & Famine Intervention, IV. Famine: Ancient & Modern Times, and V. Directories & Reports. Each of the major categories has been divided further into sections which deal with specific topics and issues. The expanded table of contents provides a useful subject index. An author index is also included for ease of locating specific works.

World Food Problems

BIBLIOGRAPHIES & REFERENCE WORKS

1. Abelson, P.H., ed. *Food: Politics, Economics, Nutrition and Research.* Washington, D.C.: American Association for the Advancement of Science, 1975.
2. Ball, Nicole. *World Hunger. A Guide to the Economic and Political Dimensions.* Santa Barbara, CA: ABC-Clio, 1981.
3. Cadet, Melissa Lawson. *Food Aid Policy for Economic Development: An Annotated Bibliography and Directory.* Sacramento, CA: Trans Tech Management Press, 1981.
4. Drasdoff, M., ed. *World Food Issues.* Ithaca, NY: Cornell University Center for the Analysis of World Food Issues, 1984.
5. Hanson, Katherine. *The World Food Problem: An Annotated Bibliography* . College Park, MD: Agricultural Experiment Station, University of Maryland, 1975.
6. Henderson, Elizabeth. *Food Aid: A Selective Annotated Bibliography on Food Utilization for Economic Development.* Rome: FAO, 1964.

7. Kent, George. *The Political Economy of Hunger: The Silent Holocaust.* New York: Praeger, 1984.
8. Myers, Melvin B. and John W. Abbott, eds. *Resource Guide on World Hunger.* New York: Council Press for Church World Service, 1968.
9. Rechcigl, Miloslav Jr. *World Food Problem: A Selective Bibliography of Reviews.* Cleveland, OH: CRC Press, 1975.
10. Talbot, Ross B. *The World Food Problem and U.S. Food Politics and Policies: 1972-1976, A Readings Book.* Ames: Iowa State University Press, 1977.
11. Talbot, Ross B., John Hawley and Julie Poorman. *Selected Bibliography on World Food Politics and Policies* . Ames: Iowa State University Press, 1985.
12. *World Food Problems: An Interdisciplinary View.* Comp. by Kenneth Marks, Gary Fouty, John Galejs, John Kawula, John McNee, Jon Pady, and Sara Pederson. Series in Bibliography No. 5. Ames: Iowa State University Library, June 1976.

U.S. GOVERNMENT REPORTS

Government reports provide information on world hunger, food supply, food relief, and food supply insurance programs. Additional subjects include hunger in developing countries, agricultural surpluses, international cooperation, and international agencies. The list below represents a small portion of available materials.

13. U. S. House. Select Committee on Hunger. Hearings; *Alleviating Hunger: Progress and Prospects.* Serial No. 98-2. 98th. Cong. 2d Sess. Washington, D.C.: GPO, June 26, 1984.
14. U. S. House. Committee on Foreign Affairs. Report; *Feeding the World's Population: Developments in the Decade Following the World Food Conference of 1974.* Congressional Research Service, Library of Congress. Washington, D.C.: GPO, 1984.
15. U. S. House. Committee on Foreign Affairs and the Select Committee on Hunger. Hearings; *World Food and Population Issues; Emergency Assistance to Africa.* 98th Cong., 2d Sess. Washington, D.C.: GPO, 1985.
16. U. S. House. Committee on Foreign Affairs. Hearings; *The World Food Situation.* 98th Cong., 1st Sess. July 26 and 27, 1983. Washington, D.C.: GPO, 1983.
17. U. S. General Accounting Office. Report; *World Hunger and Malnutrition Continue: Slow Progress in Carrying Out World Food Conference Objectives.* Washington, D.C.: GPO , 1980.

WORLD FOOD PROBLEMS: SURVEYS OF THE ISSUES

Peterson [33] points out that the poor, the diseased, the illiterate and the unemployed are a "global majority." Aziz [18] gives dimension to issues raised at the 1974 World Food Conference in Rome; the "Declaration of the Rome Forum" is reproduced. Berardi [19] collects more than 50 recent articles which provide different perspectives on world food problems. Murdoch [32] discusses the interrelationships among population growth, food supply, and poverty. The essays in Byron [22] suggest that poverty is the basic cause of world hunger; George [26] and Lappé & Collins [29, 30] argue that world food problems are a product of maldistribution, not of food shortages. The studies in Duncan [25] review the problems associated with world food shortages and world hunger and the efforts to alleviate them.

18. Aziz, Sartaj, ed. *Hunger, Politics and Markets: The Real Issues in the Food Crisis*. New York: New York University Press, 1975.
19. Berardi, Gigi M., ed. *World Food, Population and Development*. Totowa, NJ: Rowman & Allanheld, 1985.
20. Bergeson, Helge Ole. "A New Food Regime: Necessary but Impossible." *International Organization* 34 (Sp. 1980): 285-305.
21. Brown, David W. "The World Food Situation." *World Health* (Oct. 1984): 22-24.
22. Byron, William, ed. *The Causes of World Hunger*. New York: Paulist Press, 1982.
23. Christensen, Cheryl. "World Hunger: A Structural Approach." *International Organization* 32 (Su. 1978): 745-74.
24. De Marco, Susan and Susan Sechler. *The Fields Have Turned Brown: Four Essays on World Hunger*. Washington, D.C.: Agribusiness Accountability Project, 1975.
25. Duncan, E.R., ed. *Dimensions of World Food Problems*. Ames: Iowa State Free Press, 1977.
26. George, Susan. *How the Other Half Dies: The Real Reasons for World Hunger*. London: Penguin, 1976.
27. Griffin, Keith. *International Inequality and National Poverty*. New York: Holmes & Meier, 1978.
28. Harrison, Gail Grigsby. "Strategies for Solving World food Problems." In *Nutrition, Food, and Man*, pp. 141-52. Paul B. Pearson and Richard Greenwell, eds. Tucson: University of Arizona Press, 1980.
29. Lappé, Frances Moore and Joseph Collins. *Food First: Beyond the Myth of Scarcity*. Boston: Houghton Mifflin, 1977.
30. _____. *World Hunger: Ten Myths*. San Francisco: Institute For Food and Development Policy, 1982.
31. Madeley, John. "Hunger 1984." *International Relations* 8 (May 1984): 23-30.
32. Murdoch, William W. *The Poverty of Nations: The Political Economy of Hunger and Population*. Baltimore: Johns Hopkins University Press, 1980.
33. Peterson, Bill. "The Global Majority: An American Odyssey." *Washington Post*, May 14, 1978, p. A1; May 15, 1978, p.A1, A6; May 16, 1978, p. A1, A8; May 17, 1978, p. A1, A10; May 18, 1978, p. A1, A22; May 19, 1978, p. A1, A12.
34. Poleman, Thomas T. "World Food: A Perspective." *Science* 188 (May 9, 1975): 510-18.

35. Russell, Sir John E. and Norman C. Wright, eds. *Hunger: Can it be Averted?* London: British Association for the Advancement of Science, 1961.
36. Ruttan, Vernon W. "Food Crisis?" *Society* 17 (Sept.-Oct. 1980): 18-67. A series of articles about the state of food production and consumption, agriculture, and rural development in poor countries.
37. Seebohm, Frederic. "World Hunger." *African Affairs* 83 (Jan. 1984): 3-9.
38. Timmer, C. Peter, Walter P. Falcon and Scott Pearson. *Food Policy Analysis.* Baltimore: Johns Hopkins University Press, 1983.
39. Valdés, Alberto, ed. *Food Security for Developing Countries.* Boulder, CO: Westview, 1981.
40. Wilson, Charles Morrow. *The Fight Against Hunger.* New York: Funk & Wagnalls, 1969.
41. "The World Food Situation." *American Economic Review* 73 (May 1983): 235-48. Articles by G. Edward Schuh, John W. Mellor and Malcolm D. Bale, and Ronald C. Duncan.
42. Wortman, Sterling and Ralph W. Cummings, Jr. *To Feed This World.* Baltimore: Johns Hopkins University Press, 1978.

WORLD HUNGER: MORAL ISSUES

World Food Conference representatives resolved in 1974 that: "Every man, woman and child has the inalienable right to be free from hunger and malnutrition in order to develop fully and maintain their physical and mental facilities." Nicholson & Nicholson [55] explain different views on the statement. Aiken & La Follette [43] support the concept of a "right to food", while Hardin [49, 50] seeks an end to food aid because it benefits selfish interests, diminishes prospects for self-reliance, and does nothing to encourage population control. Capps & Minear [47] question the targets for aid. Gergen and Gergen [48] and Krauthammer [52] observe that aid recipients distrust America's "humanitarian" motives in providing assistance, and are suspicious of the political, economic and military objectives which they believe are the true reasons for American aid.

43. Aiken, William and Hugh La Follette, eds. *World Hunger and Moral Obligations.* Englewood Cliffs, NJ: Prentice-Hall, 1977.
44. Atwater, Tim. "The International Monetary Fund and the Third World." *Hunger* No. 22 (Feb. 1980): 1-4
45. Booher, Donald C. "Famine: An American Dilemma?" Ph.D. diss., Johns Hopkins University, 1975.
46. "Cancun." A Summit of World Leaders. Oct. 22-23, 1981. From the Report of the Independent Commission on International Issues (The Brandt Commission), 1980. *A Shift in the Wind* No. 11, Oct., 1981.
47. Capps, Carol and Larry Minear. "Development Assistance Under Fire: A Review of the Issues." *Hunger* No. 19 (Aug. 1979): 1-4.
48. Gergen, Kenneth J. and Mary M. Gergen. "What Other Nations Hear When the Eagle Screams." *Psychology Today* 8 (June 1974): 52-58.
49. Hardin, Garrett. "Lifeboat Ethics. The Case Against Helping the Poor." *Psychology Today* 8 (Sept. 1974): 38-41, 123-126.

50. _____. "The Toughlove Solution." *Newsweek* (Oct. 26, 1981): 45.

51. Islam, Nassir. "Food Aid: Conscience, Morality and Politics." *International Journal* 36 (Sp.1981): 353-70.

52. Krauthammer, Charles. "Rich Nations, Poor Nations." *New Republic* 11 (Apr. 1981): 21-23.

53. Lucas, George R. and Thomas W. Ogletree, eds., *Lifeboat Ethics: The Moral Dilemmas of World Hunger.* New York: Harper & Row, 1976.

54. Myrdal, Gunnar. "The Transfer of Technology to Underdeveloped Countries." *Scientific American* 231 (Sept. 1984): 172-82.

55. Nicholson, Heather Johnston and Ralph L. Nicholson. *Distant Hunger. Agriculture, Food, and Human Values.* West Lafayette, IN: Purdue University, 1979.

56. Pyke, Magnus. "Hunger and Humanity." *New Scientist* 67 (10 July 1975): 79-81.

57. Schertz, Lyle P. "World Food: Prices and the Poor." *Foreign Affairs* 52 (Apr. 1974): 511-537.

58. Sorenson, Vernon L. and Larry G. Hamm. "Food and Food Policy in the Industrial Nations." *Current History* 68 (June 1975): 242-44, 273-74.

DEVELOPMENT

The equation between development and progress gained popularity after World War II, when developed nations believed that their successes in utilizing technological innovations could be transferred to the entire world. Recent studies have questioned the ability of underdeveloped countries to utilize advanced technology, and many of their authors have expressed concern with growing Third World dependence upon developed nations.

59. Bauer, Peter. *Equality, The Third World and Economic Delusion.* Cambridge: Harvard University Press, 1981.

60. Eicher, Carl K. and John M. Staatz, eds. *Agricultural Development in the Third World.* Baltimore: Johns Hopkins University Press, 1984.

61. Ensminger, Douglas. "Assistance to Developing Nations." In *Dimensions of World Food Problems,* pp. 283-300. E.R. Duncan, ed. Ames: Iowa State University Press, 1977.

62. Freeman, Orville L. and Ruth Karen. "The Farmer and the Money Economy: The Role of the Private Sector in the Agricultural Development of LDC's." *Technological Forecasting and Social Change* 22 (Oct. 1982): 183-200.

63. Huddleston, Barbara. *Closing the Cereals Gap With Trade and Food Aid.* Washington, D.C.: International Food Policy Research Institute, 1984.

64. Jackson, Lady Barbara Ward and Peter Bauer. *Two Views on Aid to Developing Countries.* London: Institute of Economic Affairs, 1966.

65. Korselman, Gary H. and Kay E. Dull, eds. *Food and Social Policy.* Ames: Iowa State University Press, 1976.

122   *Famine: A Heritage of Hunger*

Economic Assistance

Hardy [71] believes that Africa's debt burden threatens even more devastating consequences than famine and that "piecemeal and short-term solutions" have been ineffective. Ayres [66] predicts that the World Bank will become more conservative as Third World problems reach "alarming" proportions.

66. Ayres, Robert L. *Banking on the Poor: The World Bank and World Poverty.* Cambridge, MA: MIT Press, 1983.
67. Barr, Terry N. "The World Food Situation and Global Grain Prospects." *Science* 214 (4 Dec. 1981): 1087-95.
68. Dadzie, K.K.S. "Economic Development." *Scientific American* 243 (Sept. 1980): 58-65.
69. Danaher, Kevin. "Banking On Hunger: The International Debt Crisis." *Food First News* No. 18 (Su. 1984): 1, 4.
70. Eberstadt, Nick. "Famine, Development and Foreign Aid." *Commentary* 79 (Mar. 1985): 25-31.
71. Hardy, Chandra. "Africa's Debt Burden." *Policy Focus* No. 5, (Sept. 1985).
72. Harle, Vilho, ed. *The Political Economy of Food.* Hants, U.K.: Saxon House, Teakfield, 1978.
73. Hopkins, Raymond and Donald J. Puchala. "Perspectives on the International Relations of Food." *International Organization* 32 (Su. 1978): 581-616.
74. Kowalewski, David. "Transnational Corporations and the Third World's Right to Eat: The Caribbean." *Human Rights Quarterly* 3 (Fall 1981): 45-64.
75. Omawale. "Nutribusiness: An Agent of the Political Economy of Hunger." *International Journal of Health Sciences* 14:2 (1984): 172-188.
76. Radice, Hugo, ed. *International Firms and Modern Imperialism.* Harmondsworth, U.K.: Penguin, 1975.

The Green Revolution

The expression "Green Revolution" describes the development of high-yield seed strains, particularly among food grains, and their application in the Third World where they have helped to increase agricultural production. Concerns have arisen regarding the high costs of new agricultural technology and the fact that governments and wealthy individuals have benefited from improved productivity, while conditions among the poorest and hungriest people in underdeveloped areas have not improved. See especially Clausen [77], Griffin [80], Morgan [84], Schuftan [86], and Greenwood & Edwards [172]. The studies in Huddleston & McLin [82] explain the magnitude of the tasks involved in extending the benefits of development to the poor. For arguments in favor of continuing technological aid, see Mellor & Adams [83].

77. Clausen, A.W. *Poverty in the Developing Countries—1985.* San Francisco: Hunger Project, 1985.

78. Cross, Michael. "Waiting for a Green Revolution." *New Scientist* 105 (4 Apr. 1985): 37-40.
79. Donders, J.G. "Putting the Famine in Context." *Commonweal* 111 (30 Nov. 1984): 658-59.
80. Griffin, Keith. *The Political Economy of Agrarian Change: An Essay on the Green Revolution.* Cambridge: Harvard University Press, 1974.
81. Güsten, Rolf. *Problems of Economic Growth and Planning: The Sudan Example.* Berlin: Springer-Verlag, 1966.
82. Huddleston, Barbara and Jon McLin. *Political Investments in Food Production. National and International Case Studies.* Bloomington: Indiana University Press, 1979.
83. Mellor, John W. and Richard H. Adams, Jr. "Feeding the Underdeveloped World: Chemical Technology is Crucial in Alleviating Poverty and Hunger." *Chemical and Engineering News* (23 Apr. 1984): 32-39.
84. Morgan, June P. "The Green Revolution in Asia: False Promise of Abundance." *Bulletin of Concerned Asian Scholars* 10 (Jan.-Mar. 1978): 2-7.
85. Muller, Mike. "Aid, Corruption and Waste." *New Scientist* 64 (7 Nov. 74): 398-400.
86. Schuftan, Claudio. "Foreign Aid and its Role in Maintaining the Exploitation of the Agricultural Sector." *International Journal of Health Services* 13:1 (1983): 33-49.
87. Taylor, Lance, Alexander H. Sarris and Philip C. Abbott. "Food Security for the World's Poor." *Technology Review* 80 (Feb. 1978): 44-54.
88. Woolley, D.G. "Food Crops—Production, Limitations, and Potentials." In *Dimensions of World Food Problems*, pp. 153-71. E.R. Duncan, ed. Ames: Iowa State University Press, 1977.

Case Studies

Falcon [91] argues that American development assistance since the 1970s has been ineffective. Shepherd [100] concludes that twenty years of Western assistance to Africa have done little to help and much to harm Africa's ability to achieve self-sufficiency. Lancaster [95] notes that drought in Africa during the 1980s focused world attention on the human tragedy of famine, but that the "deeper and more pervasive tragedy" lies in declining living standards, rising debts and an absence of resources. Ball [89] notes that ninety percent of all "natural" disasters occur in underdeveloped countries, but that aid and development programs are based on economic policies designed to benefit rich industrial countries.

89. Ball, Nicole. "The Myth of the Natural Disaster." *Ecologist* 5 (Dec. 1975): 368-71.
90. Dorner, Peter. "Land Ownership and Tenure." In *Dimensions of World Food Problems*, pp. 90-104. E.R. Duncan, ed. Ames: Iowa State University Press, 1977.
91. Falcon, Walter P. "Recent Food Policy Lessons From Developing Countries." *American Journal of Agricultural Economics* 66 (May 1984): 180-85.

92. Fischer, Lloyd K. "Constraints to Change—Social, Political and Economic." In *Dimensions of World Food Problems*, pp. 202-17. E.R. Duncan, ed. Ames: Iowa State Free Press, 1977.
93. Hartmann, Betsy and James K. Boyce. *Needless Hunger: Voices from a Bangladesh Village*. San Francisco: Institute For Food and Development Policy, 1979.
94. Kirkpatrick, Jeane J. "Africa's Economic Crisis." *Department of State Bulletin* 85 (Jan. 1985): 48-49.
95. Lancaster, Carol. "Update: Africa's Food and Development Crisis." *Policy Focus* No. 8 (Feb. 1985).
96. Lateef, Noel V. *Crisis in the Sahel: A Case Study in Development Cooperation*. Boulder, CO: Westview, 1980.
97. Low, Helen C. "Africa's Struggle for Sustained Development." *Care Briefs* No. 5 (1985): 1-12.
98. "North Africa." *Current History* 84 (May 1985): 193-240. Articles by eight specialists on the problems faced by North African governments and on U.S. policies in the region.
99. Paulino, Leonardo A. and John W. Mellor. "The Food Situation in Developing Countries: Two Decades in Review." *Food Policy* 9 (Nov. 1984): 291-303.
100. Shepherd, Jack. "When Foreign Aid Fails." *Atlantic Monthly* 255 (Apr. 1985): 41-56.
101. Walker, Gary and Frank Ballance. "Africa's Development Crisis: Looking Beyond the Famine." *Policy Focus* No.3 (July 1984).
102. Weinbaum, Marvin G. *Food, Development and Politics in the Middle East*. Boulder, CO: Westview, 1981.

U.S. OFFICIAL AID: PROGRAMS & POLICIES

The U. S., Canada, Argentina and Australia are major grain exporting countries and the U.S. is the world's largest food donor, see Vengroff & Yung [117]. Brown & Shue [103] explain the history of U.S. aid programs and the debates as to whether aid should consist of food or money. Cathie [104] contends that food aid is constrained by its effects on commercial agricultural trading interests, and believes that "untied" financial aid would permit recipient countries to choose whether they needed food or development assistance. Giacomo [106] argues that America has used food aid as a foreign policy tool. Wallerstein [118] assesses U.S. food aid policies in light of the need to reduce grain surpluses, provide a barrier against Communism, and rebuild political allies. Rothschild [111, 112] argues that the doctrine "food is power" is deceptive, because it promises an "impossible" form of influence, and nurtures a false view of what happened during the food crises of the 1970s, of the political consequences of the crisis, and of worse consequences to come.

103. Brown, Peter G. and Henry Shue, eds. *Food Policy: The Responsibility of the United States in the Life and Death Choices*. New York: Free Press, 1977.
104. Cathie, John. *The Political Economy of Food Aid*. New York: St. Martins', 1982.

105. Garzon, José. "Food Aid as a Tool of Development." *Food Policy* 9 (Aug. 1984): 232-47.
106. Giacomo, Carol. "Food For Peace." *Journal of Defense and Diplomacy.* 3 (Apr. 1985): 23-27.
107. Goulet, Denis and Michael Hudson. *The Myth of Aid.* New York: IDOC North America, 1971.
108. Hopkins, Raymond F. "The Evolution of Food Aid: Towards a Development First Regime." *Food Policy* 9 (Nov. 1984): 345-62.
109. Hopkins, Raymond and Donald J. Puchala. *Global Food Inter-dependence: Challenge to American Foreign Policy.* New York: Columbia University Press, 1980.
110. Mahoney, Mark A. "U.S. Food Aid as a Foreign Policy Instrument." In *Controversial Nutrition Policy Issues*, pp. 155-74. Georgio Solimano and Sally Lederman, eds. Springfield, IL: Charles C. Thomas , 1983.
111. Rothschild, Emma. "Food Politics." *Foreign Affairs* 54 (Jan. 1976): 285-307.
112. _____. "Is it Time to End Food For Peace?" *New York Times Magazine* (13 Mar. 1977): 15, 43-48.
113. "Senate Votes 98-1 To Clear $669 Million in African Famine Aid." *Wall Street Journal,* 21 Mar. 1985, p. 60.
114. Stanley, Robert G. *Food For Peace. Hope and Reality of U.S. Food Aid.* New York: Gordon & Breach, 1973.
115. Toma, Peter A. *The Politics of Food For Peace: Executive-Legislative Interaction.* Tucson: University of Arizona Press, 1967.
116. U. S. Foreign Aid Legislation. Public Law 480 and Title XII. *Famine Prevention and Freedom From Hunger.* Washington, D.C.: GPO, 1974 and 1975.
117. Vengroff, Richard and Yung Mei-tsai. "Food, Hunger and Dependency: PL 480 Aid to the Third World." *Journal of Asian and African Studies* 17 (July & Oct. 1982): 250-65.
118. Wallerstein, Mitchel B. *Food for War/Food for Peace? U.S. Food Aid in a Global Context.* Cambridge, MA: MIT Press, 1980.

NON-GOVERNMENT FOOD & DEVELOPMENT AID

Curti [119] provides an excellent overview of American voluntary aid; the studies in Smith & Elkin [125] explore political implications of voluntarism in underdeveloped countries. Hopcraft [120], Jones [121], and Whitaker [127] describe Oxfam work. Linden [122] and Sommer [123, 124] raise questions regarding the role, impact and future of voluntary groups. Thompson [126] believes that voluntary institutions are constrained by their lack of political power and influence.

119. Curti, Merle. *American Philanthropy Abroad: A History.* New Brunswick, NJ: Rutgers University Press, 1963.
120. Hopcraft, Arthur. *Born to Hunger.* Boston: Houghton Mifflin, 1968.
121. Jones, Mervyn. *In Famine's Shadow: A Private War on Hunger.* Boston: Beacon, 1965.

122. Linden, Eugene. *The Alms Race: The Impact of Voluntary Aid Abroad.*
New York: Random House, 1976.
123. Sommer, John G. *Beyond Charity: U.S. Voluntary Aid for a Changing
World.* Washington, D.C.: Overseas Development Council, 1977.
124. _____. *U.S. Voluntary Aid to the Third World: What is its
Future?* Washington, D.C.: Overseas Development Council, 1975.
125. Smith, David H. and Frederick Elkin, eds. *Volunteers, Voluntary
Associations and Development.* Leiden: E.J. Brill, 1981.
126. Thompson, Seth B. "International Organizations and the Improbability of
A Global Food Regime." In *Food Politics*, pp. 191-206. David Balaam
and Michael J. Carey, eds. Totowa, NJ: Allanheld, Osmun, 1981.
127. Whitaker, Ben. *A Bridge of People: A Personal View of Oxfam's First
Forty Years.* London: Heinemann, 1983.

POLITICS OF FOOD

Discussions on the politics of food pervade the literature on world food
problems; only a few examples of which are listed here. Paarlberg [132] denys
that the U.S. has used food as a foreign policy weapon, while Balaam & Carey
[128] assert that politics usually play an important role in food aid. Hopper
[130] calls the politics of food the politics of economic development and
growth as well as the politics of interactions between rich and poor nations.
See also Griffin [27, 80], Scrimshaw [187], Firebrace [406], Giacomo [106],
Mahoney, [110], and Vengroff & Yung [117].

128. Balaam, David and Michael J. Carey, eds. *Food Politics: The Regional
Conflict.* Totowa, NJ: Allanheld, Osmun, 1981.
129. Brown, Lester. *The Global Politics of Resource Scarcity.* Washington,
D.C.: Overseas Development Council, 1974.
130. Hopper, W. David. *The Politics of Food.* Ottawa, Canada: International
Development Research Centre, 1977.
131. Laird, Roy D. and Betty A. Laird. "Food Policies of Governments." In
Dimensions of World Food Problems, pp. 233-49. E.R. Duncan, ed.
Ames: Iowa State University Press, 1977.
132. Paarlberg, Robert L. *Food Trade and Foreign Policy: India, the Soviet
Union and the United States.* Ithaca, NY: Cornell University Press,
1985.

POPULATION & WORLD FOOD SUPPLY

Appleman [133] reprints Malthus as well as discussions on population
issues. Brown [135] and Ehrlich [140] propose vigorous population control
measures, while Chamberlain [136] and Simon & Hudson [153, 154] argue
that population pressure will stimulate innovations designed to support more
people. Boserup [134] observes that population growth stimulates changes in
food production and diet. Coale [137] discusses the demographic transition, but
believes that present growth rates have "impossible consequences." ul Haq
[142] argues that radical allocation of global resources is needed before

population can be controlled. Mamdani [148] and Murdoch [32] are among the many scholars who fear excessive population growth, but who do not believe that it can be controlled without broad political, economic, and social changes on behalf of people for whom large families are an economic necessity. Hardin [143] believes that rising population renders common use of resources impossible without environmental damage and examines the tragedy of the commons as a theory of population. Omran [149] notes that better health and greater longevity enhance fertility, but that reduced risks to infants tend to reduce overall reproduction.

133. Appleman, Philip, ed. *Thomas Robert Malthus: An Essay on the Principle of Population. Text Sources and Background Criticism.* New York: Norton, 1976.
134. Boserup, Ester. *The Conditions of Agricultural Growth: The Economics of Agrarian Change Under Population Pressure.* Chicago: Aldine, 1965.
135. Brown, Lester R. *The Twenty-Ninth Day.* New York: Norton, 1978.
136. Chamberlain, Neil W. *Beyond Malthus: Population and Power.* New York: Basic Books, 1970.
137. Coale, Ansley J. "The History of the Human Population." *Scientific American* 231 (Sept. 1974): 40-51.
138. Demeny, Paul. "The Populations of the Underdeveloped Countries." *Scientific American* 231 (Sept. 1974): 148-59.
139. Dietsch, Robert W. "Famine: Malthus Resurrected." *New Republic* 170 (6 Apr. 1974): 11-12.
140. Ehrlich, Paul. *The Population Bomb.* New York: Ballantine, 1968.
141. Freedman, Ronald and Bernard Berelson. "The Human Population." *Scientific American* 231 (Sept. 1974): 30-39.
142. ul Haq, Mahub. "The Food Crisis is Manageable." In *Hunger, Politics and Markets: The Real Issues in the Food Crisis,* pp. 44-47. Sartaj Aziz, ed. New York: New York University Press, 1975.
143. Hardin, Garrett. "The Tragedy of the Commons." *Science* 162 (13 Dec. 1968): 1243-48.
144. Heisel, Donald. "Food and Population in Africa." *Current History* 68 (June 1975): 258-61, 278, 288.
145. Hofsten, Erland. "Population Growth—A Menace to What?" *International Journal of Health Services* 5:3 (1975): 417-24.
146. Johnson, D. Gale. "Population, Food and Economic Adjustment." *American Statistician* 28 (1974): 89-93.
147. Knowles, John H. "Food and Population." In *Hunger, Politics and Markets: The Real Issues in the Food Crisis,* pp. 65-71. Sartaj Aziz, ed. New York: New York University Press, 1975.
148. Mamdani, Mahmood. *The Myth of Population Control: Family, Caste, and Class in an Indian Village.* New York: Monthly Review Press, 1972.
149. Omran, Abdel R. "The Epidemiologic Transition. A Theory of the Epidemiology of Population Change." *Milbank Memorial Fund Quarterly* 49 (Oct. 1971): 509-38.
150. Rechcigl, Miloslav. *Man, Food and Nutrition.* Cleveland, OH: CRC Press, 1973.

151. Revelle, Roger. "Food and Population." *Scientific American* 231 (Sept. 1974): 160-70.
152. Sai, Fred T. "The Population Factor in Africa's Development Dilemma." *Science* 226 (16 Nov. 1984): 801-5.
153. Simon, Julian L. "World Food Supplies." *Atlantic Monthly* 248 (July 1981): 72-76.
154. Simon, Julian L. and William J. Hudson. "Global Food Prospects: Good News." *Challenge* 25 (Nov.-Dec. 1982): 40-52.
155. Weyland, John. *The Principles of Population and Production.* (1816) New York: Agustus M. Kelly, 1969. Reprint.

CLIMATE, ECOLOGY & FOOD SUPPLY

Climatic variability occurs according to three phenomena: normal expected fluctuations, rare and major events, and long-term trends. Protection against normal fluctuations can be provided by dams, wells, controlled use of water resources, and flexible agricultural practices. Great floods and prolonged droughts require national and international cooperation to mitigate their effects. Long-term climatic trends are difficult to predict, but controls over deforestation and the use of fossil fuels, and cooperative research and reporting on changes, can prevent depletion of resources, provide for new resources, and establish warning systems. Le Roy Ladurie [156] examines the long-term effects of climatic change; Post [157] interjects political, economic, and social variables. Rotberg & Rabb [158] explore the entire spectrum of relationships between climate and history.

Historical Studies

156. Le Roy Ladurie, Emmanuel. *Times of Feast, Times of Famine: A History of Climate Since the Year 1000.* Garden City, NY: Doubleday, 1971.
157. Post, John D. "Meteorological History." *Journal of Interdisciplinary History* 3 (Sp. 1973): 721-32.
158. Rotberg, Robert I. and Theodore K. Rabb, eds. *Climate and History: Studies in Interdisciplinary History.* Princeton, NJ: Princeton University Press, 1981.

Climate & Food Supply

Biswas & Biswas [160] warn against ecological destruction in the process of filling human needs; while Bryson & Murray [161, 162] predict that climate is worsening. Canby [163] explains climatic change in the early 1980s and notes that wealthy nations suffered economic setbacks while poor nations experienced severe deprivation.

159. Bach, Wilfred, Jurgen Pankrath and Stephen H. Schneider. *Food-Climate Interactions: Proceedings of an International Workshop Held in West Berlin December 9-12, 1980.* Boston: D. Reidel, 1981.

160. Biswas, Margaret R. and Asit K. Biswas, eds. *Food, Climate and Man.* New York: Wiley, 1979.
161. Bryson, Reid A. "The Lessons of Climatic History." *Ecologist* 6 (July 1976): 205-11.
162. Bryson, Reid A. and Thomas J. Murray. *Climates of Hunger: Mankind and the World's Changing Weather.* Madison: University of Wisconsin Press, 1977.
163. Canby, Thomas Y. "El Nino's Ill Wind." *National Geographic* 165 (Feb. 1984): 144-83.
164. Gribbon, John. "Climate and the World's Food." *New Scientist* 64 (28 Nov. 1974): 643-45.

Ecology & Food Supply

The problems of providing increased food supplies, while causing ecological damage, are discussed in Brown [165, 166], and in Cutler [169].

165. Brown, Lester R. "Global Food Prospects: Shadow of Malthus." *Challenge* 24 (Jan.-Feb. 1982): 14-21.
166. _____. "Human Element, Not Drought, Causes Famine." *U.S. News and World Report* 98 (25 Feb.1985): 71-72.
167. _____. *State of the World 1984. A Worldwatch Institute Report on Progress Toward a Sustainable Society.* New York: Norton, 1985.
168. Carefoot, Garnet L. and E.R. Sprott. *Famine on the Wind: Man's Battle Against Plant Disease.* Chicago: Rand McNally, 1967.
169. Cutler, M. Rupert. "The Peril of Vanishing Farmlands." *New York Times*, 1 July 1980, p. A:19.
170. Dreyfus, Letha. "Can Anything Be Done? *Hunger Notes* 10 (Feb. 1985): 2-9.
171. Eckholm, Erik and Lester R. Brown. "The Spreading Desert." *War on Hunger* Pt I, vol. 11 (Aug. 1977): 1-11; Pt II, (Sept.-Oct. 1977): 1-8.
172. Greenwood, Ned H. and J.M.B. Edwards. *Human Environments and Natural Systems: A Conflict of Dominion.* North Scituate, MA: Duxbury, 1973.
173. Hayes, Dennis. *Rays of Hope.* New York: Norton, 1970.
174. Lee, John and Ronald A. Taylor. "Ravage in the Rain Forests." *U.S. News and World Report* 100 (31 Mar. 1986): 61-62.
175. MacLeod, Norman D. "Dust in the Sahel: Cause of Drought?" In *The Politics of Natural Disaster,* pp. 214-31. Michael Glantz, ed. New York: Praeger, 1976.
176. Parrack, Dwain W. "Ecosystems and Famine." *Ecology of Food and Nutrition* 7:1 (1978): 17-21.
177. Pimentel, David and Elinore Cruze Terhune. "Energy Use in Food Production." In *Dimensions of World Food Problems,* pp. 67-68. E.R. Duncan, ed. Ames: Iowa State University Press, 1977.
178. Richards, Paul. "Ecological Change and the Politics of African Land Use." *African Studies Review* 26 (June 1983): 1-83.
179. Smil, Vaclav. *The Bad Earth: Environmental Degradation in China.* New York: M.E. Sharpe, 1984.
180. "State of the Earth." *Natural History* 94 (Apr. 1985): 51-86.

181. Tinker, John, Lloyd Timberlake and Renee Sabatier. "Environmental Degradation and Human Conflict." *Alternatives* 12 (Sp.-Su. 1985): 3-7.
182. Wijkman, Anders and Lloyd Timberlake. *Natural Disasters: Acts of God or Acts of Man?* Washington, D.C.: Earthscan, 1984.
183. Wolf, Edward D. and Lester R. Brown. "Seeds of Hope in a Dying Land." *Audubon* 87 (Mar.1985): 104-7.

World Hunger

NUTRITION & HEALTH CARE

Austin [184], Evans et. al. [189], and Gwatkin et. al. [190] discuss the merits of small-scale health programs in underdeveloped countries. Berg [185, 186] and Berg et. al. [187] emphasize the detrimental effects of failures of nutrition and health interventions, and their inhibiting effects upon development programs.

184. Austin, James E. *Nutrition Programs in the Third World: Cases and Readings*. Cambridge, MA: Oelgeschlager, Gunn & Hain, 1981.
185. Berg, Alan D. *Malnourished People: A Policy View*. Poverty and Basic Needs Series. Washington, D.C.: World Bank, June 1981.
186. _____. *The Nutrition Factor: Its Role in National Development*. Washington, D.C.: Brookings Institution, 1973.
187. Berg, Alan, Nevin S. Scrimshaw and David L. Call, eds. *Nutrition, National Development, and Planning*. Cambridge, MA: MIT Press, 1973.
188. Dwyer, Johanna T. and Jean Mayer. "Beyond Economics and Nutrition: The Complex Basis of Food Policy."*Science* 188 (9 May 1975): 566-70.
189. Evans, John R., Karen Leshman Hall and Jeremy Warford. "Health Care in the Developing World: Problems of Scarcity and Choice." *New England Medical Journal* 305 (5 Nov. 1981): 1117-27.
190. Gwatkin, Davidson R., Janet R. Wilcox and Joe D. Wray. *Can Health and Nutrition Interventions Make a Difference?* Washington, D.C.: Overseas Development Council, 1980.
191. Pearson, Paul B. "World Nutrition: An Overview." In *Nutrition, Food and Man*, pp. 1-10. Paul B. Pearson and Richard Greenwell, eds. Tucson: University of Arizona Press, 1980.
192. Schmitt, Bernard A. *Protein, Calories, and Development: Nutritional Variables in the Economics of Developing Countries*. Boulder, CO: Westview, 1979.
193. Solimano, Georgio R. and Sally Lederman. *Controversial Nutrition Policies*. Springfield, IL: Charles C. Thomas, 1983.
194. Underwood, Barbara A., ed. *Nutrition Intervention Strategies in National Development*. New York: Academic Press, 1983.
195. World Health Organization. *Primary Health Care—The Chinese Experience. Report of an Inter-regional seminar*. Geneva: WHO, 1983.

PROVIDING NUTRITION & HEALTH CARE

Amsalem [196] and Jelliffe & Jelliffe [202] explain the detrimental effects of discouraging breast feeding. Marshall [203], Muñoz de Chavez [205] and Cleaver [200] examine the social and economic effects of failures in health care and the benefits of successful programs.

196. Amsalem, Tamar. "Bottle Babies: A Critical Examination of a Public Controversy." In *Controversial Nutritional Policies*, pp. 328-53. Georgio R. Solimano and Sally Lederman, eds. Springfield, IL: Charles C. Thomas, 1983.
197. Berg, Alan. "Malnutrition and Development." *Foreign Affairs* 46 (Oct. 1967): 126-36.
198. Brown, Roy E. *Starving Children: The Tyranny of Hunger*. New York: Springer, 1977.
199. Calloway, Doris Howes. "World Calorie/Protein Needs." In *Nutrition, Food, and Man*, pp. 82-87. Paul B. Pearson and Richard Greenwell, eds. Tucson: University of Arizona Press, 1980.
200. Cleaver, Harry. "Malaria and the Political Economy of Public Health." *International Journal of Health Services* 7:4 (1977): 577-79.
201. György, Paul and O.L. Kline, eds. *Malnutrition is a Problem of Ecology*. Basel, Switzerland, 1970.
202. "Hunger." (editorial) *America* 149 (12 Nov. 1983): 281-82.
203. Jelliffe, Derrick and E.F. Patrice Jelliffe. "Human Milk, Nutrition, and the World Resource Crisis." *Science* 188 (May 1975): 557-60.
204. Marshall, Carter. "Health, Nutrition, and the Roots of World Population Growth." *International Journal of Health Services* 4:4 (1974): 677-90.
205. Muñoz de Chavez, Miriam. "Malnutrition: Socio-Economic Effects and Policies in Developing Countries." In *Nutrition, Food, and Man*, pp. 38-45. Paul B. Pearson and Richard Greenwell, eds. Tucson: University of Arizona Press, 1980.

HUNGER & HUNGER-RELATED DISEASES IN HISTORY

The studies listed below provide an introduction to the combined use of historical documents and present-day understanding to explain hunger and disease in the past.

206. Aymard, Maurice. "Toward the History of Nutrition: Some Methodological Remarks." In *Food and Drink in History*, pp. 1-16. Robert Forster and Orest Ranum, eds. Baltimore: Johns Hopkins University Press, 1979.
207. Forster, Robert and Orest Ranum, eds. *Biology of Man in History*. Baltimore: Johns Hopkins University Press, 1975.
208. _____. *Food and Drink in History*. Baltimore: Johns Hopkins University Press, 1979.
209. Prentice, E. Parmalee. *Hunger and History*. New York: Harper, 1939.
210. Robson, J.R.K., ed. *Food, Ecology and Culture. Readings in the Anthropology of Dietary Practices*. New York: Gordon & Breach, 1980.

211. Rotberg, Robert I. and Theodore K. Rabb, eds. *Hunger and History: The Impact of Changing Food Production and Consumption Patterns on Society.* Cambridge: Cambridge University Press, 1983.

HUNGER & INFECTIOUS DISEASES IN HISTORY

Aykroyd [212] and Chick [213] describe the quest to understand and find cures for nutritional disorders. Henschen [214] and McNeill [215] provide similar accounts of diseases in history. The studies by Roe [216] and Williams [217] explain the histories of pellagra and beriberi.

212. Aykroyd, Wallace. *Conquest of Deficiency Diseases: Achievements and Prospects.* Geneva: WHO, 1970.
213. Chick, Harriette. "The Discovery of Vitamins." *Progress in Food and Nutrition Science*   1:1 (1975): 1-20.
214. Henschen, Folke. *The History and Geography of Diseases.* New York: Delacorte, 1966.
215. McNeill, William H. *Plagues and Peoples.* New York: Anchor, 1976.
216. Roe, Daphne A. *A Plague of Corn.* Ithaca, NY: Cornell University Press, 1973.
217. Williams, Robert R. *Toward the Conquest of Beriberi.* Cambridge: Harvard University Press, 1961.

NUTRITIONAL DISORDERS & INFECTIOUS DISEASES

Berkow [219] provides medical information on nutritional and infectious disorders. Scarpia & Kiefer [228] explain nutrient requirements. Passmore [223] sets forth U. N. recommendations for adequate food intake in lay terms. Vitamin deficiency diseases are explained in Marks [220]; Beaton & Benoga [218] discuss efforts to achieve cures on a global scale. Jean Mayer's studies [221, 222] encompass many aspects of hunger, including starvation, while the collections edited by Pearson & Greenwell [225], Rechcigl [226] and Solimano & Lederman [229] offer different perspectives on the relationships between nutrition and health.

218. Beaton, G.H. and J.M. Benoga, eds. *Nutrition and Preventive Medicine.* Geneva: WHO, 1976.
219. Berkow, Robert M., ed. *The Merck Manual of Diagnosis and Therapy.* 13th ed. New Jersey: Merck, Sharp & Dohme Research Labs., 1977.
220. Marks, John. *A Guide to the Vitamins: Their Role in Health and Disease.* Lancaster, U.K.: Medical & Technical Publishing, 1975.
221. Mayer, Jean. "Dimensions of Human Hunger." *Scientific American* 235 (Sept. 1976): 40-49.
222. _____. *Human Nutrition.* Springfield, IL: Charles C. Thomas, 1972.
223. Passmore, R. *Handbook on Human Nutritional Requirements.* Rome: FAO 1974.
224. Passmore, R. and S. Davidson. *Human Nutrition and Dietetics.* Baltimore: Williams and Wilkins, 1963.

225. Pearson, Paul B. and Richard Greenwell, eds. *Nutrition, Food, and Man: An Interdisciplinary Perspective.* Tucson: University of Arizona Press, 1980.
226. Rechcigl, Miloslav. *Man, Food and Nutrition.* Cleveland, OH: CRC Press, 1973.
227. Sanjur, Diva. *Social and Cultural Perspectives in Nutrition.* Edgewood Cliffs, NJ: Prentice-Hall, 1982.
228. Scarpia, Ionnis S. and Helen Chilton Kiefer. *Source Book on Food and Nutrition.* Chicago: Marquis Academic Media, 1978.
229. Solimano, Georgio R. and Sally A. Lederman, eds., *Controversial Nutrition Policies.* Springfield, IL: Charles C. Thomas, 1983.

MALNUTRITION: VITAMIN & MINERAL DEFICIENCIES

Available data for the incidence of vitamin and mineral deficiency disorders in different parts of the world are summarized in the following materials which emphasize the problems associated with malnutrition, and explain the difficulties in eliminating them.

230. Bailey, K.V. "Malnutrition in the African Region." *WHO Chronicle* 29 (1975): 354-64.
231. "The Fight Against Malnutrition in the World." *WHO Chronicle* 31 (1977): 276-78.
232. "The Five Principal Deficiency Diseases in the World Today."*World Health* (May 1977): 16-17.
233. György, Paul and O.L. Kline, eds. *Malnutrition is a Problem of Ecology.* Basel Switzerland: S. Karger, 1970.
234. Oomen, H.A.P.C. "Vitamin A Deficiency, Xerophthalmia, and Blindness." *Nutrition Reviews* 32 (June 1974): 161-66.
235. Pettis, Susan T. "The Eyes of the Innocent." *World Health* (Jan. 1983): 11-13.
236. Pharaon, H.M. "The Influence of Ecological Factors on Malnutrition in the Middle East." In *Malnutrition is a Problem of Ecology,* pp. 73-81. Paul György and O.L. Kline, eds. Basel, Switzerland: S. Karger, 1970.
237. Thylefors, Björn. "Avoidable Blindness." *World Health* (Jan. 1983): 2-3.
238. Truswell, A. Stewart. "Malnutrition in the Third World." *British Medical Journal* 291, Pt I (24 Aug. 1985): 525-28; Pt II (31 Aug. 1985): 587-89.
239. Urvina, Sally. "Malnutrition in Third World Countries."*Christian Century* 101 (23 May 1984): 550-52.

UNDERNUTRITION: CALORIC DEFICIENCIES & PARASITIC DISEASES

Problems associated with parasitic disorders and their effects on both nutrition and development are emphasized in the selections listed below. Virtually every author calls for collaborative research, funding for investigations, vaccine development, and programs designed to teach preventive measures.

240. Beisel, William R. "Synergism and Antagonism of Parasitic Diseases and Malnutrition." *Reviews of Infectious Diseases* 4 (July-Aug. 1982): 746-50.
241. Calloway, Doris Howes. "Nutritional Requirements in Parasitic Disease." *Reviews of Infectious Diseases* 4 (July-Aug. 1982): 891-95.
242. Crompton, David W.T. and M.C. Nesheim. "Malnutrition's Insidious Partner." *World Health* (Mar. 1984): 18-21.
243. _____. "Nutritional Science and Parasitology: A Case for Collaboration." *Bioscience* 32 (Sept. 1982): 677-80.
244. Farthing, Michael J.G. and Gerald T. Keusch. "Gut Parasites: Nutritional and Immunological Interactions." In *Nutrition, Disease and Immune Function*, pp. 87-112. Ronald Ross Watson, ed. New York: Marcel Dekker, 1984.
245. Harper, A.E., P.R. Payne, and J.C. Waterlow. "Human Protein Needs." *Lancet* 1:7818 (30 June 1973): 1518.
246. Horn, Joshua. *Away With All Pests*. New York: Monthly Review Press, 1969.
247. Rosenberg, Irwin H. and Barbara B. Bowman. "Intestinal Physiology and Parasitic Disease." *Reviews of Infectious Diseases* 4 (July-Aug. 1982): 763-67.
248. Scrimshaw, Nevin and Vernon R. Young. "The Requirements of Human Nutrition." *Scientific American* 253 (Sept. 1976): 50-64.
249. Variyam, Easwaran and John G. Banwell. "Hookworm Disease: Nutritional Implications." *Reviews of Infectious Diseases* 4 (July-Aug. 1982): 830-33.
250. Verm, Ray A. "Gastrointestinal Parasites." Part I, Protozoal Infections. *American Family Physician* 25 (Apr. 1982): 170-75.
251. ____. "Gastrointestinal Parasites." Part II, Helminthic Infections. *American Family Physician* 25 (May 1982): 216-25.

HUNGER & INFECTIOUS DISEASES

The relationship between hunger and infectious diseases is especially important among people who suffer the effects of chronic hunger. The items below emphasize potentially deadly links.

252. Bullock, Carole. "Though Spared Ethiopia's Drought, Half of Malawi's Children Die by Age Five." *Medical Tribune*, 24 July 1985, pp. 24-25.
253. Chandra, R.K. "Nutrition as a Critical Determinant in Susceptibility to Infection." *World Review of Nutrition and Dietetics* 25 (1976): 166-88.
254. Chandra, R.K. and P.M. Newberne. *Nutrition, Immunity, and Infection: Mechanisms of Interaction.* New York: Plenum, 1977.
255. Faulk, W. Page, E.M. De Mayer and A.J.S. Davies. "Some Effects of Malnutrition on the Immune Response in Man." *American Journal of Clinical Nutrition* 27 (June 1974): 638-46.
256. Gopalan, C. and G. Srikantia. "Nutrition and Disease." *World Review of Nutrition and Dietetics* 16 (1973): 97-140.

257. Lewin, Dr. Roger. "The Poverty of Undernourished Brains." *New Scientist* 64 (24 Oct. 1974): 268-71.
258. Scrimshaw, Nevin S. "Nutrition and Infection." *Progress in Food and Nutrition Science* 1:6 (1975): 393-420.
259. Scrimshaw, N.S., C.E. Taylor and J.E. Gordon. *Interactions of Nutrition and Infections.* WHO Monograph Series No. 57. Geneva: WHO, 1968.
260. Sieber, Otto F. Jr. and Glenn Lippman. "Nutrition, Infection and Immunity." In *Nutrition, Food and Man*, pp. 21-37. Paul B. Pearson and Richard Greenwell, eds. Tucson: University of Arizona Press, 1980.
261. Taylor, C.E. and Cecile De Sweemer. "Nutrition and Infection." *World Review of Nutrition and Dietetics* 16 (1973): 203-25.
262. Watson, Ronald Ross, ed. *Nutrition, Disease and Immune Function.* New York: Marcel Dekker, 1984.

HUNGER & FERTILITY

Frisch [264] asserts that "hard living" affects the ability to bear children. Bongaarts [263] and Menken et. al. [266] argue that only the severest forms of malnutrition effect fecundity and fertility. Le Roy Ladurie [265] applies scientific understanding to a disorder associated historically with starvation.

263. Bongaarts, John. "Does Malnutrition Affect Fertility? A Summary of Evidence." *Science* 208 (9 May 1980): 564-69.
264. Frisch, Rose E. "Population, Food Intake and Fertility." *Science* 199 (6 Jan. 1978): 22-30.
265. Le Roy Ladurie, Emmanuel. "Famine Amenorrhoea (Seventeenth-Twentieth Centuries)" In *Biology of Man in History*, pp. 163-78. Robert Forster and Orest Ranum, eds. Baltimore: Johns Hopkins University Press, 1975.
266. Menken, Jane, James Trussell, and Susan Watkins. "The Nutrition and Fertility Link: An Evaluation of the Evidence." *Journal of Interdisciplinary History* 11 (Winter 1981): 425-41.

STARVATION & STARVATION-RELATED DISORDERS

The most comprehensive study on starvation and starvation-related disorders is by Keys et. al. [272]. Aykroyd [267] explains the effects of prolonged hunger during famines. Cahill [269] and Young & Scrimshaw [279] provide technical data. The article by Williams [278] was the foundation for subsequent research into the problems of kwashiorkor; the results of later investigations are in Brock & Autret [268] and Trowell et. al. [275]. Viteri & Pineda [276] and Whitehead [277] explain the disorders associated with extreme undernutrition, and the problems of treating them.

267. Aykroyd, Wallace. "Definition of Different Degrees of Starvation." In *Famine*, pp. 17-22. Gunnar Blix, Yngve Hofvander and Bo Vahlquist, eds. Uppsala: Almqvist & Wiksells, 1971.
268. Brock, J.F. and M. Autret. *Kwashiorkor in Africa.* Geneva: WHO, 1952.

269. Cahill, George F. Jr. "Physiology of Acute Starvation in Man." In *Famine*, pp. 51-60. John Robson, ed. New York: Gordon & Breach, 1981.
270. _____. "Starvation in Man." *New England Journal of Medicine* 282 (Mar. 1970): 668-75.
271. De Mayer, E.M. *Protein-Energy Malnutrition*. WHO Monograph Series No. 62. Geneva: WHO, 1976.
272. Gopalan, C. and Kamala Krishnaswamy. "Famine Oedema." *Progress in Food and Nutrition Science* 1:3 (1973): 207-24.
273. Keys, Ancel, Josef Brozek, Austin Henschel, Olaf Mickelson and Henry Longstreet Taylor. *The Biology of Human Starvation*. Minneapolis: University of Minnesota Press, 1960.
274. Landman, J. and A.A. Jackson. "The Role of Protein Deficiency in the Aetiology of Kwashiorkor." *West Indian Medical Journal* 19 (Dec. 1980): 229-38.
275. Trowell, H.C., J.N.P. Davies and R.F.A. Dean. *Kwashiorkor*. London: Edward Arnold, 1954.
276. Viteri, F.E. and O. Pineda. "Effects On Body Composition and Body Function. Psychological Effects." In *Famine*, pp. 25-40. Gunnar Blix, Yngve Hofvander and Bo Vahlquist, eds. Uppsala: Almqvist & Wiksells, 1971.
277. Whitehead, R.G. "The Causes, Effects and Reversibility of Protein-Calorie Malnutrition." In *Famine*, pp. 41-51. Gunnar Blix, Yngve Hofvander, and Bo Vahlquist, eds. Uppsala: Almqvist & Wiksells, 1971.
278. Williams, Cicely D. "A Nutritional Disease of Childhood Associated With A Maize Diet." *Archives of Disease in Childhood* 8 (1933): 423-33.
279. Young, Vernon Rand Nevin S. Scrimshaw. "The Physiology of Human Starvation." *Scientific American* 225 (Oct. 1971): 14-21.

STARVATION & EPIDEMIC DISEASES

Appleby [280, 281] and Post [285] question the links between starvation and epidemic diseases in pre-modern famines; MacArthur [284] explains medical disorders among famine victims in Ireland. Foege [283] provides an excellent summary of the "triad" of disorders which precipitate the outbreak of epidemic diseases during famines. Both historians and scientists agree that political, economic, and social factors play important roles in producing epidemics during famines.

280. Appleby, Andrew. "Disease or Famine? Mortality in Cumberland and Westmorland 1580-1640." *Economic History Review*. Second Series 26 (Aug. 1973): 403-31.
281. _____. "Famine, Mortality and Epidemic Disease, A Comment." *Economic History Review* 30 (Aug. 1977): 508-13.
282. _____."Nutrition and Disease: The Case of London, 1550-1750" *Journal of Interdisciplinary History* 6 (Su. 1975): 1-17.
283. Foege, William H. "Famine, Infections and Epidemics." In *Famine*, pp. 64-73. Gunnar Blix, Ingve Hofvander, and Bo Vahlquist, eds. Uppsala: Almqvist & Wiksells, 1971.

284. MacArthur, Sir William P. "Medical History of the Famine." In *The Great Famine,* pp. 263-318. R. Dudley Edwards and T. Desmond Williams, eds. New York: New York University Press, 1957.
285. Post, John D. "Famine, Mortality and Epidemic Disease in the Process of Modernization." *Economic History Review* 29 (Feb. 1976): 14-37.

Famine & Famine Intervention

Historical surveys of famines are in Aykroyd [286] and Dando, [288, 289]. See also 273, 380, 381, 382. Aykroyd believes that the severity of famines will diminish in the future because of technology and communications; Dando predicts that it will increase because of human failures. Robson [294] includes discussions on many dimensions of famine causes, effects and history. Masefield's work [292] summarizes famine problems and offers proposals for famine prevention.

286. Aykroyd, Wallace. *The Conquest of Famine.* New York: Dutton, 1975.
287. Charbanneau, Hubert and André Larose, eds. *The Great Mortalities: Methodological Studies of Demographic Crises in the Past.* Liege: Ordina Editions, 1979.
288. Dando, William. *The Geography of Famine.* New York: Wiley, 1980.
289. _____. "Six Millennia of Famine: Map and Model." *Proceedings of the Association of American Geographers* 8 (1976): 29-32.
290. Latham, Michael C. "A Historical Perspective." In *Nutrition, Infection and National Planning,* pp. 313-28. Alan Berg, Nevin S. Scrimshaw and David L. Call, eds. Cambridge, MA: MIT Press, 1973.
291. McCance, R.A. "Famines of History and of Today." *Proceedings of The Nutrition Society* 34 (Dec. 1975): 161-72.
292. Masefield, Geoffrey. *Famine: Its Prevention and Relief.* London: Oxford University Press, 1963.
293. Nicol, B.M. "Causes of Famine in the Past and in the Future." In *Famine,* pp. 10-15. Gunnar Blix, Yngve Hofvander, and Bo Vahlquist, eds. Uppsala: Almqvist & Wiksells, 1971.
294. Robson, John R.K., ed. *Famine: Its Causes, Effects and Management.* New York: Gordon & Breach, 1981.

ISSUES & THEORIES

Many of the difficulties of defining and declaring famine, and the problems of relief, are detailed in Alamgir [295, 296], Currey [298], and Sen [304, 305]. Garcia & Garcia and Escudero [300, 301] use the Sahel as a backdrop for presenting diverse views on famine problems and for raising controversial questions regarding population growth, climatic variations, humanitarian relief, and government intervention in creating and mitigating famine conditions. Greenough [259] explores responses to famine in India and compares them with other cultures. Spitz [306] asks why people who work the land suffer most from famine.

295. Alamgir, Mohiuddin. "An Approach Towards a Theory of Famine." In *Famine*, pp. 19-40. John Robson, ed. New York: Gordon & Breach, 1981.
296. Alamgir, Mohiuddin. *Famine in South Asia: The Political Economy of Mass Starvation*. Cambridge, MA: Oelgschlager, Gunn & Hain, 1980.
297. Cox, G.W. "The Ecology of Famine: An Overview." In *Famine*, pp. 5-18. John Robson, ed. New York: Gordon & Breach, 1981.
298. Currey, Bruce. "The Famine Syndrome: Its Definition for Relief and Rehabilitation in Bangladesh." *Ecology of Food and Nutrition* 7:2 (1978): 87-98.
299. Currey, Bruce and Graeme Hugo, eds. *Famine as a Geographical Phenomenon*. Dordrecht, Holland: D. Reidel, 1984.
300. Garcia, Rolando. *Drought and Man*. Vol. I: *Nature Pleads Not Guilty*. New York: Pergamon, 1981.
301. Garcia, Rolando and José Escudero. *Drought and Man*. Vol. II: *The Constant Catastrophe: Malnutrition, Famines and Drought*. New York: Pergamon, 1982.
302. Greenough, Paul R. *Prosperity and Misery in Modern Bengal: The Famine of 1943-1944*. New York: Oxford University Press, 1982.
303. Seaman, John and Julius Holt. "Markets and Famines in the Third World." *Disasters* 4:3 (1980): 283-97.
304. Sen, Amartya. "Famines." *World Development* 8 (Sept. 1980): 613-21.
305. ————. *Poverty and Famines: An Essay on Entitlement and Deprivation*. Oxford: Oxford University Press, 1981.
306. Spitz, Pierre. "Silent Violence: Famine and Inequality." *International Social Science Review* 30:4 (1978): 867-92.

POPULAR RESPONSES TO FAMINE

Dirks [309] surveys literature on responses to acute food deficit. Den Hartog [308] discusses consumption of famine foods and comments on the importance of understanding food habits in famine-stricken areas. On famine foods, see also 483, 589. Brooks [307], Irvine [310], and Simoons [313, 314] offer insights into dietary changes in response to food deficit, while Jelliffe & Jelliffe [312] explore social consequences.

307. Brooks, Reuben H. "Human Response to Recurrent Drought in Northeastern Brazil." *Professional Geographer* 23 (Jan. 1971): 40-44.
308. Den Hartog, Adel. "Adjustment of Food Behavior During Famine." In *Famine*, pp. 155-61. John Robson, ed. New York: Gordon & Breach, 1981.
309. Dirks, Robert. "Social Responses During Severe Food Shortages and Famine." *Current Anthropology* 21 (Feb. 1980): 21-44.
310. Irvine, F.R. "Supplementary and Emergency Food Plants of West Africa." *Economic Botany* 6:1 (1952): 23-40.
311. Isto, E. "The Hungry of Brazil." *World Press Review* 30 (Nov. 1983): 55.
312. Jelliffe, Derrick and E.F. Patrice Jelliffe. "The Effects of Starvation on the Function of the Family and of Society." In *Famine*, pp. 54-61. Gunnar

Blix, Yngve Hofvander, and Bo Vahlquist, eds. Uppsala: Almqvist & Wiksells, 1971.

313. Simoons, Frederick J. "Fish As Forbidden Food: The Case of India." *Ecology of Food and Nutrition* 3:3 (1974): 185-201.
314. _____."Rejection of Fish as Human Food in Africa: A Problem in History and Ecology." *Ecology of Food and Nutrition* 3:2 (1974): 89-105.
315. Sorokin, Pitirim A. *Man and Society in Calamity: The Effects of War, Revolution, Famine, Pestilence Upon Human Mind, Behaviour, Social Organization and Cultural Life.* New York: Dutton, 1942.

RELIEF & PREVENTION

Famine intervention is explained in Blix et. al. [316, 325, 328, 336, 337, 341, 343, 346, 347, 349], Currey [319], and Robson [294]. Dow [320], Sheets & Morris [331], Wade [332], and Wiseberg [333] criticize relief operations in the Sahel, provide insights into the obstacles confronted by official and private relief organizations, and offer recommendations for improvements. Chen & Northrup [317] and Kapsiotis [322] argue that relief does not affect underlying disorders. They, along with Mayer [327], suggest methods for improving famine intervention and measures for famine prevention. Claiborne [318] advocates food banks as insurance against crop failures. Scrimshaw [330], among others, favors long-term development programs to prevent famines. Pirie [329] outlines political and social difficulties which stand in the way of change.

316. Blix, Gunnar, Yngve Hofvander, and Bo Vahlquist, eds. *Famine: A Symposium Dealing With Nutrition and Relief Operations in Times of Disaster.* Uppsala: Almqvist & Wiksells, 1971.
317. Chen, Lincoln and Robert S. Northrup. "Framework for Disaster Relief." In *Disaster in Bangladesh*, pp. 257-73. Lincoln C. Chen, ed. New York: Oxford University Press, 1973.
318. Claiborne, Robert. "Weathering the Lean Years." *Saturday Review* 4 (13 Nov. 1976): 20-22, 24.
319. Currey, Bruce. "Coping With Complexity in Food Crisis Management." In *Famine As A Geographical Phenomenon*, pp. 183-202. Bruce Currey and Graeme Hugo, eds. Dordrecht, Holland: D. Reidel, 1984.
320. Dow, Thomas E. "Famine in the Sahel: A Dilemma for United States Aid." *Current History* 68 (May 1975): 197-201.
321. Food and Agricultural Organization of the United Nations. *Drought in the Sahel: International Relief Operations, 1973-1975. A Report.* Rome: FAO, 1975.
322. Kapsiotis, G.D. "An International Programme for Famine Relief." *Proceedings of The Nutrition Society* 34 (Dec. 1975): 195-99.
323. Masefield, Geoffrey. *Food and Nutrition Procedures in Times of Disaster.* FAO Nutrition Series No. 21. Rome: FAO, 1967.
324. Mayer, Jean. "Coping With Famine." *Foreign Affairs* 53 (Oct. 1974): 98-120.

140   *Famine: A Heritage of Hunger*

325. _____. "Famine Relief." In *Famine,* pp. 178-88. Gunnar Blix, Yngve Hofvander, and Bo Vahlquist, eds. Uppsala: Almqvist & Wiksells, 1971.
326. _____. "Management of Famine Relief." *Science* 188 (9 May 1975), 573-76.
327. _____. "Preventing Famine." *Science* 227 (15 Feb. 1985): 707.
328. Passmore, R. "Famine Relief." In *Famine,* pp. 92-93. Gunnar Blix, Yngve Hofvander, and Bo Vahlquist, eds. Uppsala: Almqvist & Wiksells, 1971.
329. Pirie, N.W. "Some Obstacles to Eliminating Famine." *Proceedings of The Nutrition Society* 34 (Dec. 1975): 181-86.
330. Scrimshaw, Nevin S. "The Politics of Starvation." *Technology Review* 87 (Aug.-Sept. 1984), 18-26.
331. Sheets, Hal and Roger Morris. *Disaster in the Desert. Failures of International Relief in the West African Drought.* Washington, D.C.: Carnegie Endowment for International Peace, 1974.
332. Wade, Nicholas. "Sahelian Drought: No Victory for Western Aid." *Science* 185 (19 July 1974): 234-37.
333. Wiseberg, Laurie. "An International Perspective on the African Famines." In *The Politics of Natural Disaster,* pp. 101-27. Michael H. Glantz, ed. New York: Praeger, 1976.

CASE STUDIES: FOOD & MEDICAL RELIEF

Specific measures for providing relief to famine victims are discussed below. Sabry [348] provides criteria for assessing physical status among famine victims. The FAO report [339] focuses on post-emergency feeding problems. Aall [334], Ifekwunigwe [341], and Omololu [347] criticize the lack of experience, poor coordination, and inappropriate relief supplies which characterized relief operations in Nigeria and recommend improvements. Berg's study on relief operations in Bihar [336] offers examples of successful relief management. Bang [335] emphasizes the need for disease control which, he believes, "must compete" with food, clothing, shelter, and water. May [344, 345, 369] provides a journalistic view of famine relief work in Ethiopia. Only a few of his many articles for the *New York Times* are cited.

334. Aall, C. "Relief, Nutrition and Health in the Nigerian Biafran War." *Journal of Tropical Pediatrics* 16:2 (1970): 69-90.
335. Bang, Frederik B. "The Role of Disease in the Ecology of Famine." In *Famine,* pp. 61-75. John Robson, ed. New York: Gordon & Breach, 1982.
336. Berg, Alan. "Famine Contained: Notes and Lessons From the Bihar Experience." In *Famine,* pp. 113-29. Gunnar Blix, Yngve Hofvander, and Bo Vahlquist, eds. Uppsala: Almqvist & Wiksells, 1971.
337. Benoga, J.M. "Nutritional Rehabilitation Under Emergency Conditions." In *Famine,* pp. 84-89. Gunnar Blix, Yngve Hofvander, and Bo Vahlquist, eds. Uppsala: Almqvist Wiksells, 1971.

338. Cuny, Frederick C. "Issues In the Provision of Food Aid Following Disasters." In *Famine*, pp. 89-94. John Robson, ed. New York: Gordon & Breach, 1981.
339. Food and Agricultural Organization of the United Nations. *Management of Group Feeding Programs*. Rome: FAO, 1982.
340. Hay, Roger W. "The Concept of Food Supply System With Special Reference to the Management of Famine." In *Famine*, pp. 81-88. John Robson, ed. New York: Gordon & Breach, 1981.
341. Ifekwunigwe, Aaron. "Recent Field Experiences in Eastern Nigeria (Biafra)." In *Famine*, pp. 144-54. Gunnar Blix, Ingve Hofvander and Bo Vahlquist, eds. Uppsala: Almqvist & Wiksells, 1971.
342. Manetsch, Thomas J. "On Strategies and Programs for Coping With Large Scale Food Shortages." In *Famine*, pp. 95-104. John Robson, ed. New York: Gordon & Breach, 1981.
343. Masefield, Geoffrey. "Calculations of the Amounts of Different Foods to be Imported in the Famine Area—Emergency Subsistence Level; Temporary Subsistence Level." In *Famine*, pp. 170-75. Gunnar Blix, Yngve Hofvander and Bo Vahlquist, eds. Uppsala: Almqvist & Wiksells, 1971.
344. May, Clifford. "The Famine Workers." *New York Times Magazine* (1 Dec.1985): 60-62, 70.
345. _____. "Field Notes on the Psychology of Famine." *New York Times*, 9 June 1985, IV, 9:1.
346. Monckeberg, F. "Treatment of Severe Infant Malnutrition." In *Famine*, pp. 74-82. Gunnar Blix, Yngve Hofvander and Bo Vahlquist, eds. Uppsala: Almqvist & Wiksells, 1971.
347. Omololu, Dr. A. "Nutrition and Relief Operations—The Nigerian Experience." In *Famine*, pp. 130-35. Gunnar Blix, Yngve Hofvander and Bo Vahlquist, eds. Uppsala: Almqvist & Wiksells, 1971.
348. Sabry, Z.I. "Assessing the Nutritional Status of Populations." *Food and Nutrition* 3:4 (1977): 2-6.
349. Teply, L.J. "What Kinds of Foods Should Primarily Be Provided, Particularly for Young Children, In Famine? In *Famine*, pp. 165-69. Gunnar Blix, Yngve Hofvander and Bo Vahlquist, eds. Uppsala: Almqvist & Wiksells, 1971.
350. de Ville de Goyet, C., J. Seaman and N. Geijer. *The Management of Nutritional Emergencies in Large Populations*. Geneva: WHO, 1978.

DISASTER OPERATIONS & REFERENCE WORKS

Disaster studies examine such events as great floods, earthquakes and volcanic eruptions, and describe how societies respond. Although they do not address famines as separate events, they offer insights into the nature of relief operations and organizations. Ahearn [351] and Manning [359] address problems confronted by relief organizations. Baker & Chapman [352] emphasize potential uses of modern science and technology in disaster response. Brown [354] notes that about ninety percent of relief for "natural disasters" in underdeveloped countries is food aid which is difficult to deliver, diminishes incentives to renew local food production, and often is inadequate.

142   *Famine: A Heritage of Hunger*

Turner [365] and Cuny [355] believe that most disasters are preventable. Like Brown [354], Cuny [355] is concerned that assistance ultimately might further exacerbate poverty, or reverse progress toward self-reliant development. Green [357] comments on the unwillingness of governments to admit disaster problems, notes that past relief has been undertaken without forethought, and predicts worse future disaster situations. Rorholt [361] believes that many of the criticisms of disaster relief operations are justified, and suggests advanced planning.

351. Ahearn, Frederick L. Jr. and Raquel E. Cohen. *Disasters and Mental Health: An Annotated Bibliography.* Rockville, MD: National Institute of Mental Health, 1984.
352. Baker, George W. and Dwight Chapman, eds. *Man and Society in Disaster.* New York: Basic Books, 1962.
353. Ball, Nicole. "The Myth of the Natural Disaster." *Ecologist* 5 (Dec. 1975): 368-71.
354. Brown, Barbara. *Disaster Preparedness and the U.N. Advance Planning for Disaster Relief.* New York: Pergamon, 1979.
355. Cuny, Frederick C. *Disasters and Development.* New York: Oxford University Press, 1983.
356. Forsythe, David. "Diplomatic Approaches to the Political Problems of International Relief in Natural Disasters." In *Disaster Assistance,* pp. 267-92. Lynn H. Stephens and Stephen J. Green, eds. New York: New York University Press, 1979.
357. Green, Stephen. *International Disaster Relief: Toward a More Responsive System.* New York: McGraw-Hill, 1977.
358. Hewitt, Kenneth, ed. *Interpretations of Calamity From the Viewpoint of Ecology.* Boston: Allan & Unwin, 1983.
359. Manning, Dianah H. *Disaster Technology: An Annotated Bibliography.* Oxford: Pergamon, 1976.
360. National Research Council. Committee on International Disaster Assistance. *Assessing International Disaster Needs.* Washington, D.C.: National Academy of Science, 1979.
361. Rorholt, Arnold. *Pre-Disaster Planning and Organization of Disaster Assistance.* Paper distributed by the League of Red Cross Societies. Geneva: LRCS, 1972.
362. Sheets, Hal and Roger Morris. *Disaster in the Desert: Failures of International Relief in the West African Drought.* Washington, D.C.: Carnegie Endowment for International Peace, 1974.
363. Stephens, Lynn H. and Stephen J. Green, eds. *Disaster Assistance: Appraisal, Reform and New Approaches.* New York: New York University Press, 1979.
364. Taylor, Alan and Frederick Cuny. "The Evaluation of Humanitarian Assistance." *Disasters* 3:1 (1979): 37-42.
365. Turner, Barry A. *Man-made Disasters.* London: Wykeham, 1978.

FAMINE & WAR

Reports on the combined effects of famine and war punctuate historical famine accounts. [For scientific accounts on famine conditions during World War II see 273, 510, 511, 512]. One of the goals of the World Food Conference held in Rome in 1974 was to outlaw starvation as a means of warfare, but available data give no evidence that Conference resolutions have been respected during recent hostilities.

366. Bond, James E. *The Rules of Riot: Internal Conflict and the Law of War.* Princeton, NJ: Princeton University Press, 1974.
367. Davis, Morris. *Civil Wars and the Politics of International Relief.* New York: Praeger, 1975.
368. Henderson, Peggy L. and Robin J. Biellik. "Comparative Nutrition and Health Services for Victims of Drought and Hostilities in the Ogaden: Somalia and Ethiopia, 1980-1981." *International Journal of Health Services* 13:2 (1983): 289-306.
369. May, Clifford. "War Rivals Drought in Africa's Hunger Crisis." *New York Times,* 29 Sept. 1985, I, 13:1.
370. Mayer, Jean. "Famine in Biafra." *Postgraduate Medicine* 45 (Apr. 1969): 236-40.
371. Mudge, George B. "Starvation as a Means of Warfare." *International Lawyer* 4:2 (1970): 228-68.

RED CROSS, U. S. & U. N. RELIEF EFFORTS

Dulles' study [372] of the American Red Cross (ARC) provides an overview of history, goals and world-wide relief operations. Forsythe [373] explains the role of the International Committee of the Red Cross (ICRC) and surveys ICRC and ARC functions. Holdsworth [374] examines criticisms directed at Red Cross relief activities. Tansley [376] summarizes Red Cross proposals for improvements.

The American role in providing food for civilian victims of hostilities grew during and after World War I, when much of the relief work was supervised by Herbert Hoover [375]. United Nations plans for post- World War II food relief, as well as measures for restoring agricultural production in war-torn areas, are in the 1943 report of the U. N. Conference [377]. Woodbridge [378] chronicles UNRRA activities during the immediate post-war period.

372. Dulles, Foster Rhea. *The American Red Cross: A History.* New York: Harper, 1950.
373. Forsythe, David. *Humanitarian Politics: The International Committee of the Red Cross.* Baltimore: Johns Hopkins University Press, 1977.
374. Holdsworth, David J. *The Present Role of the Red Cross in Assistance.* Background Paper. No. 3. Geneva: International Committee of the Red Cross/League of Red Cross Societies, 1975.

375. Hoover, Herbert. *An American Epic: Famine in Forty-Five Nations. The Battle on the Front Line 1914-1923*. 4 vols. Chicago: Regnery, 1959-1964.
376. Tansley, Donald. *Final Report: An Agenda for Red Cross*. Geneva: International Committee of the Red Cross/League of Red Cross Societies, 1975.
377. U. N. Conference on Food and Agriculture. Hot Springs, VA. May 18-June 3, 1943. *Final Act and Section Reports*. Washington, D.C.: GPO, 1943.
378. Woodbridge, George. *UNRRA: A History of the United Nations Relief and Rehabilitation Administration*. New York: Columbia University Press, 1950.

Famine: Ancient & Modern Times

ANCIENT WORLD

Graves [381] and Walford [382] provide broad overviews of famines in history. Studies by Bell [383], Gapp [384], Shea [385] and Weitz [386] provide information on different episodes of famine.

379. Cohen, Mark Nathan. *The Food Crisis in Prehistory*. New Haven: Yale University Press, 1977.
380. Dando, William. *The Geography and History of Famine*. New York: Wiley, 1980.
381. Graves, Ralph. "Fearful Famines of the Past." *National Geographic* 32 (July 1917): 69-90.
382. Walford, Cornelius. *Famines of the World, Past and Present. Being Two Papers Read Before the Statistical Society of London in 1878 and 1879 Respectively, and Reprinted From its Journal, 1879*. New York: Burt Franklin, 1970. Reprint.
383. Bell, Barbara. "The Dark Ages in Ancient History. I: The First Dark Age in Egypt." *American Journal of Archaeology* 75 (Jan. 1971): 3-26.
384. Gapp, Kenneth Spencer. "The Universal Famine Under Claudius." *Harvard Theological Review* 28 (1935): 258-65.
385. Shea, William H., "Famines in the Early History of Egypt and Syro-Palestine." Ph.D. diss., University of Michigan, 1976.
386. Weitz, Daniel. "Famine and Plague as Factors in the Collapse of the Roman Empire in the Third Century." Ph.D. diss., Fordham University, 1972.

AFRICA

Famine in Africa is not a twentieth century phenomenon. Pankhurst [394] recorded episodes of widespread starvation in 1252, 1258-1259, 1261-1262, 1272-1275, 1330, 1702, 1828-1829, 1842-1843, and 1888-1892 in northeastern Africa alone. Food shortages have resulted from droughts, animal diseases and locust invasions. The decline to famine has been a product of political, economic, social and ecological disorders. Lofchie [389] and Ball

[387] call attention to political and economic disorders in producing famine conditions.

387. Ball, Nicole. "Understanding the Causes of African Famine." *Journal of Modern African Studies* 14 (Sept. 1976): 517-22.
388. Commins, Stephen K., Michael F. Lofchie and Rhys Payne, eds. *Africa's Agrarian Crisis: The Roots of Famine.* Boulder, CO: Rienner, 1985.
389. Lofchie, Michael F. "The Political and Economic Origins of African Hunger." *Journal of Modern African Studies* 13 (Dec. 1975): 551-67.
390. Muzaale, Patrick J. "Famine and Hunger in Rural East Africa: Analysis and Intervention." Ph.D. diss., University of California, Berkeley, 1980.
391. Walker, Brian. "The Famine in Africa: Causes and Solutions." *USA Today* 114 (July 1985): 38-41.

19th Century Famines

392. Dias, Jill R. "Famine and Disease in the History of Angola c.1830-1930." *Journal of African History* 22 (1981): 349-78.
393. Durrill, Wayne K. "Atrocious Misery: The African Origins of Famine in Northern Somalia, 1839-1884." *American Historical Review* 91 (Apr. 1986): 287-306.
394. Pankhurst, Richard. *The Great Ethiopian Famine of 1888-1892.* Addis Ababa: Haile Selassie I University, 1964.

Ethiopia, 1972-1973

The authors of studies on the Ethiopian famine of 1972-1973 are unanimously critical of the Ethiopian government and of the international community for not publicizing famine conditions because announcing them might have jeopardized development programs. See especially Mariam [397], and Shepherd [402].

395. Addis Ababa. Haile Selassie I University. *Famine Relief and Rehabilitation Organization. Policy and Procedure Manual and Progress Report, October 1974.* Addis Ababa: University Famine Relief and Rehabilitation Organization., 1974.
396. Love, Robert S. "Economic Change in Pre-Revolutionary Ethiopia." *African Affairs* 78 (July 1979): 339-55.
397. Mariam, Mesfin Wolde. *Rural Vulnerability to Famine in Ethiopia, 1958-1977.* Addis Ababa: Vikas Publishing House with Addis Ababa University, 1984.
398. Matthews, Christopher J. "The Road to Korem." *New Republic* 192 (21 Jan. 1985): 23-25.
399. Miller, D.S. and J.F. Holt. "The Ethiopian Famine." *Proceedings of The Nutrition Society* 34 (Dec. 1975): 167-72.
400. Nolan, Liam. *The Forgotten Famine.* Dublin: Mercier, 1974.
401. Shepherd, Jack. "Africa: Drought of the Century." *Atlantic Monthly* 253 (Apr. 1984): 36-40. ·

402. _____. *The Politics of Starvation.*   New York: Carnegie Endowment for International Peace, 1975.

Ethiopia, 1980-1986

Newspapers, magazines, and journals provided extensive coverage of the famine in Ethiopia, only a few of which are cited here. Franey [407] puts the famine in its historical context. Political and military disorders and their role in worsening famine conditions are in Hoben [408], Schwab [410], and Suau [411]. Figures for U. S. official aid are noted in Congressional reports [404, 405, 406]. Barnes [403] enumerates the problems of delivering and distributing relief. Firebrace [406] and Tucker [412] reported that aid from large institutions was used by the Ethiopian government as a weapon against rebellious Eritreans, and that Western food donations were smuggled into Sudan for sale at inflated prices.

403. Barnes, Lafayette. "Ethiopian Famine: International Response." *Congressional Research Service Review* 6 (May 1985): 5-9.
404. "Ethiopian Famine." *Congressional Research Service Bureau* 6 (May 1985): 5-9.
405. "Ethiopian Famine." *Department of State Bulletin* 85 (Mar. 1985): 28.
406. Firebrace, James. "Food as a Military Aid." *New Statesman* 107 (7 Dec. 1984): 20.
407. Franey, Ros. "Lessons to be Learned." *Drought and Famine in Ethiopia.* Report, July 1984. Boston: Oxfam America. Available from Oxfam.
408. Hoben, Allan. "The Origins of Famine." *New Republic* 192 (21 Jan. 1985): 17-19.
409. Kaplan, Robert D. "Ethiopian Exodus." *New Republic* 192 (21 Jan. 1985): 20-22.
410. Schwab, Peter. "Political Change and Famine in Ethiopia." *Current History* 84 (May 1985): 221-23, 227-28.
411. Suau, Anthony. "Region in Rebellion: Eritrea." *National Geographic* 168 (Sept. 1985): 384-405.
412. Tucker, Jonathan B. "The Politics of Famine in Ethiopia: Half May Starve." *Nation* 240 (19 Jan. 1985): 33, 45-50.

Mozambique

413. Hanlon, Joseph. "Too Little, Too Late." *New Statesman* 107 (3 Febr. 1984): 18.

Nigeria/Biafra, 1968-1969

The Nigerian civil war began in in July 1967 and lasted thirty months. The federal military government enforced a blockade in eastern Nigeria to suppress tribal uprisings. Their goal was to cause a collapse in the economy and prevent inter-regional movements of goods and money. Since imports into the eastern region consisted largely of protein foods, widespread nutritional deficiencies occurred throughout the blockaded area.

414. Apeldoorn, G. Jan Van. *Perspectives on Drought and Famine in Nigeria.* London: Allen & Unwin, 1981.
415. Du Bois, Victor D. *The Drought in Niger.* 4 vols. Hanover, NH: American Universities Field Staff, 1974.
416. Stremlau, John. *The International Politics of the Nigerian Civil War.* Princeton, NJ: Princeton University Press, 1977.
417. Watts, Michael. *Silent Violence: Food, Famine and Peasantry in Northern Nigeria.* Berkeley: University of California Press, 1983.

Nyasaland

418. Vaughan, Megan. "Famine Analysis and Family Relations: 1949 in Nyasaland." *Past and Present* No. 108 (Aug. 1985): 177-205.

The Sahel, 1969-1973

Famine in the Sahel, 1969-1973, had multiple causes. Drought caused food shortages, but the combined effects of ecological damage, underdevelopment, an absence of basic health care services, and the practice of growing cash crops for export played a major role in precipitating starvation. National and international relief operations were later criticized in numerous studies.

419. Ball, Nicole. "Drought and Dependence in the Sahel." *International Journal of Health Services* 8:2 (1978): 271-98.
420. Brown, Barbara J., Janet C. Tuthill and E. Thomas Rowe. *International Disaster Response: The Sahelian Experience.* Denver: University of Denver, 1976.
421. Bryson, R.A. "Drought in Sahelia: Who or What is to Blame?" *Ecologist* 2 (Dec. 1973): 366-71.
422. Colvin, Lucie Gallister. *The Uprooted of the Western Sahel: Quest for Cash in the Senegambia.* New York: Praeger, 1981.
423. Franke, Richard W. and Barbara H. Chasin. *Seeds of Famine: Ecological Destruction and the Development Dilemma in the West African Sahel.* Montclair, NJ: Allanheld, Osmun, 1980.
424. Glantz, Michael H. "Nine Fallacies of Natural Disaster: The Case of the Sahel." In *The Politics of Natural Disaster,* pp. 3-24. Michael H. Glantz, ed. New York: Praeger, 1976.
425. Gould, P. "Famine as a Spatial Crisis: Programming Food to the Sahel." In *Famine As A Geographical Phenomenon,* pp. 135-54. Bruce Currey and Graeme Hugo, eds. Dordrecht, Holland: Reidel, 1984.
426. Picardi, Anthony C. and William Seifert. "A Tragedy of the Commons in the Sahel." *Ekistics* 43 (May 1971): 297-304.
427. *Sahel: A Guide to the Microfiche Collection of Documents and Dissertations.* Ann Arbor, MI: University Microfilms, 1981.

428. Seaman, J., Julius Holt, and John Murlis. "An Inquiry Into the Drought Situation in Upper Volta." *Lancet* No. 7832, vol. II (Oct. 1973): 774-78.
429. Sterling, Claire. "The Making of The Sub-Saharan Wasteland." (How to spend hundreds of millions of dollars to help people starve.) *Atlantic Monthly* 233 (May 1974): 98-105.
430. Twose, Nigel. "Behind the Weather." *Why the Poor Suffer Most. Drought and the Sahel.* Report, 1984. Boston: Oxfam America. Available from Oxfam.
431. U. S. Agency for International Development. *Sahel Recovery and Rehabilitation Program, Mali: Proposal and Recommendation.* Washington, D.C.: AID, 1974.

South Africa, 1899-1902

To deny food and intelligence to Boer guerrillas, Lord Kitchener ordered the British army to burn farms and to confine Boer women and children to camps situated along railway lines. Between 20,000 and 28,000 of them died of starvation and disease, as did an estimated 175,000 black Africans.

432. Pakenham, Thomas. *The Boer War.* New York: Random House, 1979.
433. Spies, S.B. "Women and the War." In *The South African War: The Anglo-Boer War 1899-1902,* pp. 161-85. Peter Warwick, ed. New York: Longman, 1980.

Sudan, 1980s

Famine in 1984-1986 affected approximately twenty percent of Sudan's twenty-two million people. The problems of assisting them were compounded by an estimated 746,000 refugees from other famine-stricken parts of Africa. Internal civil strife, poor roads, inadequate railways, and limited air facilities further inhibited relief operations.

434. Kaplan, Robert. "Sudan: A Microcosm of Africa's Ills." *Atlantic Monthly* 257 (Apr. 1986): 20-24.
435. May, Clifford. "In West Sudan, Promised Food is Slow to Arrive." *New York Times* , 2 July 1985, I, 11:1.
436. Renner, G.T., Jr. "A Famine Zone in Africa: The Sudan." *Geographical Review* 16 (Oct. 1926): 582-96.
437. Rondos, Alex. "Civil War and Foreign Intervention in Chad." *Current History* 84 (May 1985): 209-12, 232.
438. Taha, S.A. "Ecologic Factors Underlying Protein-Calorie Malnutrition in an Irrigated Area of the Sudan." *Ecology of Food and Nutrition* 7:4 (1979): 193-201.

Tanzania

Food shortages which occurred in Tanzania during the first half of the 20th century were the product of natural and human causes. During recent years, shortages have resulted from official policies which forced farmers to sell produce to the government at fixed prices and then pay taxes on the sales.

439. Berry, L., T. Hankins, R.W. Kates, L. Make and P. Porter. "Human Adjustment to Agricultural Drought in Tanzania: Pilot Investigation." *Research Paper* No. 13. Bureau of Resource Assessment and Land Use. University of Dar es Salaam, Jan. 1971.
440. Brooke, Clarke. "Types of Food Shortages in Tanzania." *Geographical Review* 57 (July 1967): 333-57.
441. Robson, John R.K. "The Ecology of Malnutrition in a Rural Community in Tanzania." *Ecology of Food and Nutrition* 3:1 (1974): 61-72.

Uganda

Civil war and the rise to power of Idi Amin led to social unrest and widespread starvation.

442. Jaynes, Gregory. "African Apocalypse." *New York Times Magazine*. (16 Nov. 1980): 74-80, 82, 84-86.

Zaire

443. Pagezy, Helene. "Seasonal Hunger As Experienced by the Oto and the Twa of a Ntomba Village in the Equatorial Forest (Lake Tumba, Zaire)." *Ecology of Food and Nutrition* 12:3 (1982): 139-53.

CAMBODIA/KAMPUCHEA, 1979-1980,

In 1969, Cambodia was bombed by the United States military after Prince Sihanouk gave aid to North Vietnam. Sihanouk was deposed in 1970 when General Lon Nol took power. The Pol Pot regime which followed was, in turn, overthrown by Heng Samrin in 1975, with Vietnamese support. Shawcross [450] provides a critical account of foreign response to reports on famine. Mason & Brown [449] concentrate on the specific tasks of carrying out relief. Ea [446] predicts ongoing food problems.

444. Branigan, William. "Cambodia: A Fragile Convalescence." *Washington Post* (9 Aug. 1981): A1, A19; (10 Aug. 1981): A1, A19; (11 Aug. 1981): A1, A12; (12 Aug. 1981): A1, A16.
445. Capps, Carol. "Kampuchea (Cambodia) A Portrait of Famine." *Hunger* No. 21 (Dec. 1979): 1-4.
446. Ea, Meng Try. "War and Famine: The Kampuchea Example." In *Famine As A Geographical Phenomenon*, pp. 33-47. Bruce Currey and Graeme Hugo, eds. Dordrecht, Holland: Reidel, 1984.

447. Kamm, Henry. "Life in 'Liberated' Cambodia." *New York Times Magazine.* (18 May 1980): 76, 78, 80-82, 84-87.
448. Leifer, Michael. "Kampuchea 1979: From Dry Season to Dry Season." *Asian Survey* 20 (Jan. 1980): 33-41.
449. Mason, Linda and Roger Brown. *Rice Rivalry and Politics: Managing Cambodian Relief.* Notre Dame, IN: University of Notre Dame Press, 1983.
450. Shawcross, William. *The Quality of Mercy: Cambodia, Holocaust and Modern Conscience.* NewYork: Simon & Schuster, 1984.

CHINA

Li [453] summarizes Chinese traditional famine intervention, presents new approaches to the study of food and famine in Chinese history, and includes an excellent bibliography. Hsiao [452] describes the disorders which inhibited relief during the 19th century. Ho [451] discusses statistics on droughts, floods and famines and warns against erroneous conclusions about physical and human losses. See also Hosie [458, 459] and Yao [462, 463]. Mallory's study [454] is a summary drawn from work done in the 1920s by the China International Famine Relief Commission [468, 469, 470].

451. Ho Ping-ti. *Studies on the Population of China.* Cambridge: Harvard University Press, 1959.
452. Hsiao K'ung-chüan. *Rural China: Imperial Control in the Nineteenth Century.* Seattle: University of Washington Press, 1960.
453. Li, Lillian. "Introduction: Food, Famine, and the Chinese State." *Journal of Asian Studies* 41 (Aug. 1982): 687-707.
454. Mallory, Walter. *China: Land of Famine.* New York: American Geographical Society, 1926.

Historical Studies

Bohr [455] provides a comprehensive account of famine in China during the 1870s, of Chinese traditional famine relief, and of the foreign role in providing for Chinese famine victims. Insights into foreign famine relief are found in Hyatt [460].

455. Bohr, Paul Richard. *Famine in China and the Missionary: Timothy Richard as Relief Administrator and Advocate of National Reform, 1876-1884.* Cambridge: Harvard University Press, 1972.
456. Dudgeon, John Hepburn. "The Famine in North China." *Chinese Recorder* 11 (Sept.-Oct. 1880): 349-57.
457. Dunstan, Helen. "The Late Ming Epidemics: A Preliminary Survey." *Ch'ing-Shih Wen-T'i* 3 (Nov. 1975): 1-59.
458. Hosie, Alexander. "Droughts in China, A.D. 620 to 1643." *Journal of the North China Branch of the Royal Asiatic Society,* new series, 12 (1878): 51-89.

459. Hosie, Alexander. "Floods in China, A.D. 620 to 1630." *China Review* 7 (May-June 1897): 371-72.
460. Hyatt, Irwin T., Jr. "Protestant Missions in China, 1877-1890: The Institutionalization of Good Works." In *American Missionaries in China,* pp. 93-106. K.C. Liu, ed. Cambridge: Harvard University Press, 1966.
461. Legge, James, trans. *The Famine in China. Pictures Illustrating the Terrible Famine in Honan That Might Draw Tears From Iron. Extracts from a translation of the Chinese texts.* London: Kegan Paul, 1878.
462. Yao Shan-yu. "The Chronological and Seasonal Distribution of Floods and Droughts in Chinese History, 206 B.C.-A.D. 1911." *Harvard Journal of Asiatic Studies* 6 (1942): 273-312.
463. _____. "The Geographical Distribution of Floods and Droughts in Chinese History, 206 B.C.-A.D. 1911." *Far Eastern Quarterly* No. 2 (Aug. 1943): 357-78.
464. Yim Shu-yuen. "Famine Relief Statistics as a Guide to the Population of Sixteenth Century China: A Case Study of Hunan Province." *Ch'ing-Shih Wen-T'i* 3 (Nov. 1978): 1-30.

Famines, 1900-1949

Famines occurred somewhere in China almost every year during the first half of the 20th century. Deaths numbered in the millions in 1906-1907, 1911-1912, 1928-1929, and 1943. Foreign and Sino-foreign relief work between 1900-1949 is examined in Golkin [471]. For information on Red Cross operations, see entries 465, 466, 467, and 471 as well as 119 and 372. China International Famine Relief Commission goals, philosophies, and operations are explained in Nathan [474] and in entries 468, 469, 470, and 480. Famine in Honan in 1943 is described by White [481] and by White & Jacoby [482].

465. American Red Cross. *The Report of the American Red Cross Commission to China.* Washington D.C.: American National Red Cross, 1929.
466. American Red Cross. *Report of the China Famine Relief, October 1920-September 1921.* Shanghai: Commercial Press, n.d.
467. Bicknell, Ernest. *Pioneering With the Red Cross.* New York: Macmillan, 1935.
468. China International Famine Relief Commission. *Famine in China's Northwest. American Red Cross Commission's Findings and Rejoinders Thereto.* Series B, No. 41. Peiping: June 1930.
469. China International Famine Relief Commission. *Handbook for Relief Workers.* Advance Edition. Peking: Sept. 1924.
470. China International Famine Relief Commission. *Scientific Disaster Relief.* Series B, No. 28. Peking: 1928.
471. Golkin, Arline T. "The Faces of Hunger: Famine Relief to China, 1900-1949." Ph.D. diss., University of Southern California, 1984.
472. MacNair, Harley Farnsworth. *With the White Cross in China: The Journal of a Relief Worker With a Preliminary Essay by Way of Introduction.* Peking: Henry Vetch, 1939.

473. Mead, Daniel W. "Floods and Famine in China." *Journal of Geography* 14 (Mar. 1916): 261-74.
474. Nathan, Andrew James. *A History of the China International Famine Relief Commission.* Cambridge: Harvard University Press, 1965.
475. Peking United International Famine Relief Committee. *International Cooperation in Famine Relief 1920-1921. Report of the Personnel Committee of the Peking United International Famine Relief Committee.* Peking: Sept. 1921. (n.p.)
476. Peking United International Famine Relief Committee. *The North China Famine of 1920-1921 With Special Reference to the West Chihli Area. Being the Report of the Peking United International Famine Relief Committee.* Peking: Commercial Press Works, 1922.
477. Republic of China. *Report of the National Flood Relief Commission, 1930-32.* Shanghai: Comacrib Press, 1933.
478. Snow, Edgar. *The Other Side of the River.* New York: Random House, 1961.
479. Tawney, R.H. *Land and Labour in China.* New York: M.E. Sharpe, 1932.
480. Todd, Oliver J. *Two Decades in China.* Peking: Association of Chinese and American Engineers, 1938. Reprint ed. Taipei: Ch'eng-wen, 1971.
481. White, Theodore B. *In Search of History: A Personal Adventure.* New York: Harper & Row, 1978.
482. White, Theodore and Analee Jacoby. *Thunder Out of China.* New York: William Sloane, 1946.
483. Yi, L.K. and Y.Y. Ferny. "A Note on the Composition of Some Wild Leaves, Barks and Roots That May Be Used as Foodstuffs During Famine Time." *Journal of The Chinese Chemical Society* 9:2 (1942): 157-63.

Hunger & Famine, 1950-1980s

Compilations by Barnett [485] and Blair [487] explain China's development since 1949. Hsu [490] examines changes in the agricultural sector. Optimistic accounts on land use, food production and population control, such as by Stavis [493, 494], are offset by evidence of severe famine conditions in 1960-1961. See especially Bernstein [486], London & London [491], Domes [488], and Piazza [492]. Recent reports have suggested that population losses in 1960-1961 may have ranged from10 to 28 million.

484. Asian Peoples' Anti-Communist League, Republic of China. *Famine as Told by Letters From the Chinese Mainland.* Taipei, 1962.
485. Barnett, A. Doak. *China and the World Food System.*   Washington, D.C.: Overseas Development Council, 1979.
486. Bernstein, Thomas P. "Starving to Death in China." *New York Review of Books* 30 (16 June 1983): 36-38.
487. Blair, Patricia. *Development in the People's Republic of China: A Selected Bibliography.* Washington, D.C.: Overseas Development Council, 1976.

488. Domes, Jürgen. *Socialism in the Chinese Countryside: Rural Societal Policies in the People's Republic of China, 1949-1979*. Margitta Wendling, trans. London: C. Hurst, 1980.

489. Dwyer, D.J. "China's Natural Calamities and Their Consequences." *Geography* 216, Pt 3 (July 1962): 301-5.

490. Hsu, Robert C. *Food for One Billion: China's Agriculture Since 1949*. Boulder, CO: Westview, 1982.

491. London, Miriam and Ivan D. London. "The Other China." Part I: The Three Flags of Death; Part II: The Case of the Missing Beggars; "Hunger in China: The Norm of Truth. *Worldview* (May 1976): 4-11; (June 1976): 43-48; (Mar. 1979): 12-16.

492. Piazza, Alan. *Trends in Food and Nutrient Availability in China, 1950-1981*. Washington, D.C.: World Bank, 1983.

493. Stavis, Benedict. "Ending Famines in China." In *Drought and Man*, vol. 2, pp. 112-139. Rolando Garcia and Jose Escudero, eds. New York: Pergamon, 1982.

494. _____."How China is Solving its Food Problems." *Bulletin of Concerned Asian Scholars* (July-Sept. 1975): 22-38.

EAST TIMOR

After East Timor, an island 400 miles north-west of Australia, was abandoned by Portugal in 1975, conditions were characterized by civil war, invasion by Indonesia and famine. An estimated 100,000 people died.

495. Kamm, Henry. "The Silent Suffering in East Timor." *New York Times Magazine* (15 Feb. 1981): 34-35, 56, 58, 60-63.

496. Patterson, Benjamin. "The Plight of East Timor." *America* 149 (12 Nov. 1983): 288-90.

ENGLAND

497. Appleby, Andrew. *Famine in Tudor and Stuart England*. Stanford, CA: Stanford University Press, 1978.

498. Clarkson, Leslie. *Death, Disease, and Famine in Pre-Industrial England*. New York: St. Martins' , 1975.

499. Kershaw, Ian. "The Great Famine and Agrarian Crisis in England 1315-1322." *Past and Present* No. 59 (May 1973): 3-50.

EUROPEAN FAMINES

Background studies provide insights into the conditions which created vulnerability to famine and which promoted the spread of epidemic diseases.

500. Blum, Jerome. "The Condition of the European Peasantry on the Eve of Emancipation." *Journal of Modern History* 46 (Sept. 1974): 395-24.

501. Hufton, Olwen H. *The Poor of Eighteenth Century France, 1750-1789*. Oxford: Clarendon Press, 1974.

502. Lis, Catharina and Hugo Soly. *Poverty and Capitalism in Pre-Industrial Europe*. Atlantic Highlands, NJ: Humanities Press, 1979.
503. Meuvret, Jean. "Demographic Crisis in France From the Sixteenth to the Eighteenth Century." In *Population In History*, pp. 507-22. D.V. Glass and D.E.C. Eversley, eds. London: Edward Arnold, 1965.
504. Turpeinen, Oiva. "Infectious Diseases and Regional Differences in Finnish Death Rates, 1749-1773." *Population Studies* 32 (Nov. 1978): 523-33.

Historical Studies of Famines in Europe

505. Berger, Patrice M. "The Famine of 1692-1694 in France: A Study in Administrative Response." Ph.D. diss., University of Chicago, 1972.
506. Jutikkala, E. "The Great Finnish Famine in 1696-1697." *Scandinavian Economic History Review* 3:1 (1955): 48-63.
507. Jutikkala, E. and M. Kauppinen. "The Structure of Mortality During Catastrophic Years in a Pre-Industrial Society." *Population Studies* 25 (July 1971): 283-85.
508. Lucas, Henry S. "The Great European Famine of 1315, 1316, 1317." *Speculum* 5 (Oct. 1930): 343-77.
509. Post, John D. *The Last Great Subsistence Crisis in the Western World*. Baltimore: Johns Hopkins University Press, 1977.

20th Century War-Related Famines

Dols & Van Arken [510] and Stein et. al. [511] report on fetal diseases, mental retardation, and nutritional disorders associated with extreme hunger in Holland during World War II. Valaoras [512] notes that in Greece, men died in greater numbers than women, because women were protected with scarce food supplies, and that young children fared less well than older children who learned to scavenge for food.

510. Dols, M.J.L. and D.J.A.M. Van Arken. "Food Supply and Nutrition in the Netherlands During and Immediately After World War II." *Milbank Memorial Fund Quarterly* 24 (July 1946): 319-55.
511. Stein, Zena, Mervyn Susser, Gerhart Saenger and Francis Marolla. *Famine and Human Development: The Dutch Hunger Winter of 1944-1945*. New York: Oxford University Press, 1975.
512. Valaoras, V.G. "Some Effects of Famine on the Population of Greece." *Milbank Memorial Fund Quarterly* 24 (July 1946): 215-34.

INDIA

India's historical famines are surveyed in Loveday [514]. Srivastava [526] explains Famine Codes. Bhatia [513] provides an economic context for famines under British rule and argues that famines were the result of poverty. McAlpin [515] blames climatic disorders rather than British administration for famines. Together, the two studies provide meaningful insights into both famine history and historical debate. For additional background, see Alamgir [296].

513. Bhatia, B.M. *Famines in India: A Study in Some Aspects of the Economic History of India.* 2d ed. Bombay: Asia Publishing, 1967.
514. Loveday, A. *History and Economics of Famine in India.* London: Bell, 1914.
515. McAlpin, Michelle Burge. *Subject To Famine: Food Crises and Economic Change in Western India, 1860-1920.* Princeton, NJ: Princeton University Press, 1983.

Historical Studies

516. Ambirajan, Srinivasa. "Political Economy and Indian Famines." *South Asia* No.1 (Aug. 1971): 20-28.
517. Carlyle, R.W. "Famine in a Bengal District in 1896-1897." *Economic Journal* 10 (Sept. 1900): 421-30.
518. Digby, William. *The Famine Campaign in Southern India (Madras and Bombay Presidencies and Province of Mysore) 1876-1878.* London: Longmans, Green, 1878.
519. *Famine in India. (World Food Supply). Reprint of Report of the Indian Famine Commission, 1901.* Calcutta: Office of the Supt. of Govt. Print.,1901; and Sir A. Cotton. *The Madras Famine.* London: Simpkin, Marshall,1880(?). New York: Arno, 1976. Reprint.
520. Ghosh, Kali Charan. *Famines in Bengal 1770-1943.* Calcutta: Indian Associated Publishing, 1944.
521. _____. *Famines in India, 1860-1965.* Calcutta: Indian Associated Publishing, 1967.
522. Lambert, George. *India: The Horror Stricken Empire Containing a Full Account of the Famine, Plague, and Earthquake of 1896-97.* Berne, IN: Mennonite Book Concern, 1898.
523. Merewether, Francis Henry Shafton. *Famine Districts of India: A Tour Through the Famine Districts of India.* London: Innes, 1898.
524. Patnaik, Gorachand. *The Famine and Some Aspects of the British Economic Policy in Orissa, 1866-1905.* Cuttack: Vidyapuri, 1981.
525. Porter, Alexander. *The Diseases of the Madras Famine of 1877-78.* Madras: Government Press, 1889.
526. Srivastava, Hari Shanker. *The History of Indian Famines and Development of Famine Policy (1858-1918).* Agra: Sri Ram Mehtra, 1968.
527. _____."The Indian Famine of 1876-79." *Journal of Indian History* 44 (1966): 853-86.

Bengal: 1943-1944

Most studies of the Bengal famine are extremely critical of British policies. Sen [535] argues that food shortage was not a primary cause of the famine. Ela Sen [536] offers a woman's view of the famine. Pike [533] was a missionary and least critical of official actions. Studies by Alamgir [295, 296] provide both a historical and theoretical context for understanding famines in India and, especially, in Bengal. Greenough [529] incorporates historical evidence, social understanding, and sympathy for all parties.

528. Ghosh, Tushar Kanti. *The Bengal Tragedy*. Lahore: Hero Publications, 1944.
529. Greenough, Paul R. *Prosperity and Misery in Modern Bengal: The Famine of 1943-1944*. New York: Oxford University Press, 1982.
530. India. Famine Inquiry Commission. *Report on Bengal/India Famine Inquiry Commission*. (1945) New York: Arno, 1976. Reprint.
531. Mukherji, R.K. "The Effects of the Food Crisis of 1943 on the Rural Population of Noakhali, Bengal." *Science and Culture* 10:5-6 (1944): 185-91, 231-38.
532. Narayan, T.G. *Famine Over Bengal*. Calcutta: The Book Company, foreword dated March 1944.
533. Pike, Clarence Edward. *Famine: The Story of the Great Bengal Famine of 1943, of Famines Before and Famines Since, and How Their Retreat Can be Thwarted*. Cornwall, Ont., Canada: Vesta, 1982.
534. Santhanam, K. *The Cry of Distress*. New Delhi: Hindustan Times Press, 1943.
535. Sen, Amartya. "Starvation and Exchange Entitlements: A General Approach and its Application to the Great Bengal Famine." *Cambridge Journal of Economics* 1 (Mar. 1977): 33-59.
536. Sen, Ela. *Darkening Days: Being a Narrative of Famine-Stricken Bengal*. Calcutta: Susil Gupta, 1944.
537. Uppal, J.N. *Bengal Famine of 1943: A Man-Made Tragedy*. Delhi: Atma Ram, 1984.
538. Venkataramani, M.S. *Bengal Famine of 1943: The American Response*. Delhi: Vikas, 1973.

Bihar, 1966-1967

Bihar is seen as model for famine relief [336], because it had adequate transportation, improved water systems, existing development programs, and central government support for relief work. Brass [539] has criticized official unwillingness to admit famine conditions until they reached extreme proportions.

539. Brass, Paul R. "The Bihar Famine of 1966-1967." *Journal of Asian Studies* 45 (Feb. 1986): 245-67.
540. *Famine Relief and Reconstruction: Report of the Workshop (January 12-16, 1971)*. New Delhi: Central Institute of Research & Training in Public Cooperation, 1971.
541. Halse, Michael. "Food Production and Food Supply Programmes in India." *Proceedings of the Nutrition Society* 34 (1975): 173-80.
542. Ramalingaswami, V., M.G. Deo, J.S. Guleria, S.K. Sood, Om Prakash, and R.V.N. Sinha. "Studies of the Bihar Famine of 1966-1967." In *Famine*, pp. 94-110. Gunnar Blix, Yngve Hofvander, and Bo Vahlquist, eds. Uppsala: Almqvist & Wiksells, 1971.

543. Scarfe, Wendy and Allen Scarfe. *Tiger on a Rein: Report on the Bihar Famine*. London: G. Chapman, 1969.
544. Singh, Kumar Suresh. *The Indian Famine of 1967: A Study in Crisis and Change*. New Delhi: People's Publishing House, 1975.

Bangladesh, 1974

Chen [545] outlines multiple disorders which preceded and accompanied famine in 1974. Dodge & Wiebe [548] describe Oxfam relief operations. Famine food consumption and corruption in official relief administration are described in Rahman [549] and Raymer [550].

545. Chen, Lincoln M., ed. *Disaster in Bangladesh: Health Crises in a Developing Nation*. New York: Oxford University Press, 1973.
546. Chen, Lincoln C. and Jon E. Rohde. "Famine and Civil War in Pakistan." *Lancet* 2:7724 (11 Sept. 1971): 557-60.
547. Clay, Edward. "The 1974 and 1984 Floods in Bangladesh: From Famine to Food Crisis Management." *Food Policy* 10 (Aug. 1985): 202-6.
548. Dodge, Patrick Cole and Paul D. Wiebe. "Famine Relief and Development in Rural Bangladesh." *Economic and Political Weekly* 11 (29 May 1976): 809-17.
549. Rahman, M.M. "The Causes and Effects of Famine in the Rural Population: A Report From Bangladesh." *Ecology of Food and Nutrition* 7:2 (1978): 99-102.
550. Raymer, Steve. "The Nightmare of Famine." A Picture Story. *National Geographic* 148 (July 1975): 33-39.
551. Sengupta, Sunil. *Famine-Hunger-Growth: A Study of Food Situation in India*. New Delhi: New Age, 1975.

IRELAND

Famine in Ireland during the 1840s is examined by Woodham-Smith [563]. Gallagher [560] is a social history, while Mokyr [561] and O'Brien [562] focus on economic problems.

552. Edwards, R. Dudley and T. Desmond Williams, eds. *The Great Famine: Studies in Irish History 1845-52*. New York: New York University Press, 1957.
553. Green, E.R.R. "Agriculture." In *The Great Famine*, pp. 89-128. R. Dudley Edwards and T. Desmond Williams, eds. New York: New York University Press, 1957.
554. MacArthur, Sir William P. "Medical History of the Famine." In *The Great Famine*, pp. 263-318. R. Dudley Edwards and T. Desmond Williams, eds. New York: New York University Press, 1957.
555. MacDonagh, Oliver. "Irish Emigration to the United States of America and the British Colonies During the Famine." In *The Great Famine*, pp. 319-388. R. Dudley Edwards and T. Desmond Williams, eds. New York: New York University Press, 1957.

556. McDowell, R.B. "Ireland On the Eve of the Famine." In *The Great Famine*, pp. 3-86. R. Dudley Edwards and T. Desmond Williams, eds. New York: New York University Press, 1957.

557. McHugh, Roger J. "The Famine in Irish Oral Tradition." In *The Great Famine*, pp. 391-436. R. Dudley Edwards and T. Desmond Williams, eds. New York: New York University Press, 1957.

558. Nowlan, Kevin B. "The Political Background." In *The Great Famine*, pp. 131-206. R. Dudley Edwards and T. Desmond Williams, eds. New York: New York University Press, 1957.

559. O'Neill, Thomas P. "The Organisation and Administration of Relief, 1845-52." In *The Great Famine*, pp. 209-59. R. Dudley Edwards and T. Desmond Williams, eds. New York: New York University Press, 1957.

560. Gallagher, Thomas Michael. *Paddy's Lament: Ireland 1846-1847 Prelude to Hatred.* New York: Harcourt Brace Janovich, 1982.

561. Mokyr, Joel. *Why Ireland Starved: A Quantitative and Analytical History of the Irish Economy, 1800-1850.* Boston: Allen and Unwin, 1985.

562. O'Brien, George A.T. *The Economic History of Ireland from the Union to the Famine.* (1921) Clifton, NJ: A.M. Kelly, 1972.

563. Woodham-Smith, Cecil. *The Great Hunger: Ireland 1845-1849.* New York: Harper & Row, 1962.

JAPAN

564. Arakawa, H. "Meteorological Conditions of the Great Famines in the Last Half of the Tokugawa Period, Japan." *Papers on Meteorology and Geophysics* 6 (Sept. 1955): 101-16.

565. Kalland, Arne and Jon Pederson. "Famine and Population in Fukuoka Domain During Tokugawa Period." *Journal of Japanese Studies* 10 (Winter 1984): 31-72.

RUSSIA/SOVIET UNION

(1891-1892)

Robbins [569] places government response to famine conditions in a broad historical context; Dando [566] criticizes official relief efforts, and Hodgetts [567] and Queen [568] relate personal experiences.

566. Dando, W.A. "Man-Made Famines: Some Geographical Insights From an Exploratory Study of a Millennium of Russian Famines." *Ecology of Food and Nutrition* 4:4 (1976): 219-34.

567. Hodgetts, Edward A.B. *In the Track of the Russian Famine: The Personal Narrative of a Journey Through the Famine Districts of Russia.* London: T. Fisher Unwin, 1892.

568. Queen, George S. "American Relief to the Russian Famine of 1891-1892." *Russian Review* 14 (1955): 140-50.

569. Robbins, Richard G. *Famine in Russia, 1891-1892: The Imperial Government Responds to a Crisis.* New York: Columbia University Press, 1975.

570. Simms, James Y., Jr. "The Impact of the Russian Famine of 1891-92: A New Perspective." Ph.D. diss., University of Michigan, 1976.

(1921-1923)

Weissman [578] argues that American food saved an estimated ten million lives and contributed to the maintenance of the Bolshevik regime. Sorokin's manuscript [577] was written during the famine, and smuggled out of the country. Asquith [571], Fisher [573], and Goulder [574] describe foreign relief efforts.

571. Asquith, Michael. *Famine (Quaker Work in Russia, 1921-1923)*. New York: Oxford University Press, 1943.
572. Edmondson, Charles M. "Soviet Famine Relief Measures, 1921-1923" Ph.D. Diss., Florida State University, 1970.
573. Fisher, H.H. *The Famine in Soviet Russia 1919-1923: The Operations of the American Relief Administration*. Stanford, CA: Stanford University Press, 1927.
574. Goulder, F.A. and Lincoln Hutchinson. *On the Trail of the Russian Famine*. Stanford, CA: Stanford University Press, 1927.
575. Hiebert, Peter C. and Orie O. Miller. *Feeding the Hungry: Russia Famine, 1919-1921*. Scottdale, PA: Mennonite Central Committee, 1929.
576. Kennan, George. *The Decision to Intervene*. Princeton, NJ: Princeton University Press, 1958.
577. Sorokin, P.A. *Hunger as a Factor in Human Affairs*. (1922) Elena P. Sorokin, trans. Gainesville, FL: University Presses of Florida, 1975.
578. Weissman, Benjamin M. *Herbert Hoover and Famine Relief to Soviet Russia: 1921-1923*. Stanford, CA: Hoover Institution, 1974.

(1932-1934)

Famine in the Soviet Union from 1932 to 1934 resulted from ruthless government procurement policies which left the populations of affected areas with inadequate food reserves. Official refusal to halt grain exports and inadequate distribution of available grain supplies caused distress and death among millions. Government concealment of famine conditions makes it difficult to determine losses, but mortality estimates range from four to seven million.

579. Carynnyk, Marco. "The Famine The "Times" Couldn't Find." *Commentary* 76 (Nov. 1983): 32-40.
580. Chamberlain, William Henry. "The Ordeal of the Russian Peasantry." *Foreign Affairs* 12 (Apr. 1934): 495-507.
581. Dalrymple, Dana G. "The Soviet Famine of 1932-34." *Soviet Studies* 15 (Jan. 1964): 250-84; 16 (Apr. 1965): 471-74.
582. Dolot, Miron. *Execution By Hunger: A Survivor's Account of 1932-1933 in Ukraine in Which Over Seven Million People Were Deliberately Starved to Death*. New York: Norton, 1985.

583. Hryshko, Vasyl I. *The Ukrainian Holocaust of 1933.* (1933) Marco
Carynnyk, trans. & ed. Toronto: Bahriany Foundation 1983.
584. Mace, James E. "Famine and Nationalism in Soviet Ukraine." *Problems of
Communism* 33 (May-June 1984): 37-50.
585. Voropai, Oleksa. *The Ninth Circle: In Commemoration of the Victims of
the Famine of 1933.* Cambridge: Harvard University, Ukrainian Studies
Foundation, 1983.

Directories & Reports

ASSISTANCE & RELIEF

Items 586-593 provide information on organizations devoted to
alleviating world hunger. Reports and newsletters listed in entries 594-602 are
available in libraries or by direct communication.

586. Boynes, Wynta, ed. *U.S. Nonprofit Organizations in Development
Assistance Abroad.* 8th ed. New York: Technical Assistance
Information Clearing House of the American Council of Voluntary
Agencies for Foreign Service, 1983.   Lists 475 U.S. non-profit
organizations, programs, objectives, and countries of activity.
587. Development Centre of the Organisation for Economic Co-operation and
Development. *Directory of Non-Governmental Organisations in OECD
Member Countries Active in Development Co-operation.* 2 vols. Paris,
1981. Lists 1,702 organizations engaged in education and development
aid.
588. Knowles, Louis L. *A Guide to World Hunger Organizations: Who They Are
and What You Should Know About Them.*   Decatur, GA:
Seeds/Alternatives, 1984.   Analyzes some 20 organizations working to
end world hunger and engaged in relief and development.
589. Kutzner, Patricia L. and Nicola Lagoudakis, eds. *Who's Involved With
Hunger: An Organization Guide.* 4th ed. Washington, D.C.: World
Hunger Education Service, 1985.   Lists and describes more than 200
organizations.
590. Lowenstein, Florence M., ed. *Development Education Programs of U.S.
Nonprofit Organizations.* New York: Technical Assistance Information
Clearing House of the American Council of Voluntary Agencies for
Foreign Service, 1983.   Lists 108 organizations located in the U. S.;
indexed according to area of program focus.
591. The National Council for International Health (NCIH) is a nonprofit
professional organization working to strengthen United States
participation in international health, especially in developing
countries.   Information is available from National Council for
International Health, Suite 740, 2100 Pennsylvania Avenue, NW,
Washington, D.C., 20037.
592. U. S. Agency for International Development. *(AID) Voluntary Foreign Aid
Programs: Reports of American Voluntary Agencies Engaged in
Overseas Relief and Development Registered With the Agency for
International Development.* Washington, D.C.: AID, 1983.   Lists 167

non-government organizations registered with AID as eligible for AID funding and gives brief descriptions of their activities.
593. Worthington, Linda, ed. *Who's Involved With Hunger: An Organization Guide.* 4th ed. Washington, D.C.: World Hunger Education Service, 1985. Lists over 400 private organizations that are major sources of materials on education and development.

SELECTED REPORTS, REVIEWS & NEWSLETTERS

594. *Care Briefs On Development Issues.* Published by CARE in cooperation with the Overseas Development Council. Reports contain analyses of CARE operations around the world. CARE World Headquarters, 600 First Avenue, New York, NY 10016.
595. *Ceres.* A bi-monthly review published by the United Nations, FAO, which contains news and analyses of agricultural and development programs around the world.
596. *Food First News.* Published by the Institute for Food and Development Policy, 1885 Mission Street, San Francisco, CA 94103-3584. The Institute, founded in 1975 by Frances Moore Lappe and Joseph Collins, focuses on issues of food and justice around the world.
597. *Food and Nutrition.* Prepared by the Food Policy and Nutrition Division of FAO, this is a bi-annual report on world developments in nutrition, with particular reference to FAO work. Issues contain articles on research, technical assistance, education and standards in food and nutrition.
598. *Oxfam America News.* Published three times a year to provide information on world-wide Oxfam projects, along with lists of educational resources and programs for Americans on hunger and development issues. Headquarters are at Oxfam America, 115 Broadway, Boston, MA 02116.
599. *Policy Focus.* Published by the Overseas Development Council, an independent, non-profit organization established in 1969 to educate Americans on the economic and social problems confronting developing countries and to promote awareness of their importance to the U. S. in an interdependent international system. Background papers are available from Overseas Development Council, 1717 Massachusetts Ave., N.W., Washington, D.C. 20036.
600. *A Shift in The Wind.* Published by, and containing descriptions of, Hunger Project programs. Hunger Project international offices are at 1 East 42nd Street, New York, NY 10017.
601. *UNDRO News.* Published bi-monthly by the U. N. Disaster Relief Coordinator (UNDRO), Palais des Nations, 1211 Geneva 10, Switzerland. The publication lists disaster alerts, disaster emergencies, and relief operations carried out under UNDRO auspices. It is not an official document, but is designed to provide public information.
602. *World Health.* The official illustrated magazine of the U. N. World Health Organization (WHO) is published ten times a year. It covers a variety of topics including nutrition, malnutrition, immunology, and population.

Index